# *Classic*
# FRENCH
## COOKING

# *Classic*
# FRENCH
## COOKING
*Recipes for mastering the French kitchen*

ELISABETH LUARD

spruce

An Hachette Livre Company
First published in Great Britain in 2004 by Spruce,
a division of Octopus Publishing Group Ltd
2–4 Heron Quays, London E14 4JP
www.octopusbooks.co.uk

Distributed in the United States and Canada by
Hachette Book Group USA
237 Park Avenue
New York
NY 10017

ISBN-13: 978-1-84072-875-0
ISBN-10: 1-84072-875-2

10 9 8 7 6 5 4 3

Printed and bound in China

# contents

# *introduction*

The French know what they like and they know what they do well—in art, in philosophy and, above all, in the kitchen.

The recipes that define the everyday cooking of France —pâté de campagne, moules mariniére, steak au poivre, petits pois à la française, ratatouille, daube de bœuf, civet de liévre, lapin à la moutarde, gigot à l'ail, poulet à la crème, coq au vin, tarte au citron, mousse au chocolat— these are the recipes that need no translation, the ones that appear on every menu from Calais to Marseilles.

Fashions in food change—Thai today, Sicilian tomorrow —but whenever two or three food-lovers are gathered together to share a forkful of something special, France sets the standard by which all others are judged. No other tradition is as diverse, as vigorous or as capable of reinventing itself.

Happily for my infant tastebuds—endangered in youth by English boarding-school catering—I acquired my kitchen habits from a Frenchwoman, the formidable Bernadette, a cook employed by my stylish Jewish American grandmother. At the time, the early fifties, my grandmother had made the Atlantic crossing, established herself in a large house in fashionable Belgrave Square and begun the assault on London society that was the duty of every American heiress. Born in Baltimore, heiress to a large British tobacco fortune, she was married at fifteen to a gambler (her cousin, the undoing of the family finances). Hers was a glamorous lifestyle. My grandfather gambled with King Farouk and played cards with Onassis. She was a friend of the Rothschilds and the Duchess of Windsor, whose lifestyle and tastes she shared, and the exquisite French food served at her table in defiance of post-war rationing turned her into one of London's most fashionable hostesses.

Although the staff who bustled about in the cavernous subterranean kitchens included a pastry-chef and a sauce chef—maître-saucier—as well as the usual complement of underlings, it was Bernadette who really ran the show. Bernadette who conducted the daily interview with my grandmother to determine the day's menu. Bernadette who dictated what came in and what went out of the kitchen. Bernadette who badgered the butcher, bullied the fishmonger, and picked over every vegetable the greengrocer delivered. Bernadette shopped daily in Soho, bought nothing out of season, and never let anything go to waste even though, as she was fond of lamenting, it was hard to find a reliable pork-butcher who might be trusted to feed the household's edible debris to a suitable pig. The shortages of post-war London did not make her any less demanding: she would rail against the impurity of the butter, the blandness of the cream, and the unsuitability of British beef to dishes which demanded French veal.

She also ensured that I, the only granddaughter, already captivated by what went on in the kitchen, should acquire the basics of what, in her view, every young girl should know. This included how to tell the exact degree of doneness of a grilled entrecôte by testing it with your thumb; how to stop a béchamel from going lumpy by ensuring the liquid added was always boiling; how to judge the precise moment at which an omelete should be tipped out of the pan in order that it should be served baveuse—frothy within, firm without. Bernadette cooked instinctively, with the certainty of those who understand exactly why and what they do. And when my arm ached from beating the butter and sugar that went into her quatre-quarts—the French version of the English pound cake—she wouldn't let me set the bowl down until she had herself decided the mixture had achieved an acceptable lightness. She wrote nothing down and never ever, as far as I was aware, consulted a book or made a list. Looking back, it is quite possible she could neither read nor write; but she could cook and run a kitchen. My grandmother had to pay her more than any chef, though she told me this in the strictest confidence—as a matter of pride, she explained, rather than greed.

Happily, I was allowed to spend as much time in Bernadette's kingdom as I pleased. And pleasure—not perfection, not even the exact reproduction of a recipe— was what she sought to give. She had little respect for written recipes, dismissing them as largely unworkable, and saw no point in expensive ingredients if they did not, in her view, add to the enjoyment of what she cooked. She would cheerfully alter any recipe to suit the ingredients she had to hand. Her only rule was that if the ingredient was good when it came into the kitchen, all you had to do was not spoil it.

Later, as a teenager, I would join my grandmother in the various fashionable watering places where my grandfather played the tables. Monte Carlo, Montecatini, Eugénie les Bains, Marienbad, Deauville, and Paris were all places where the rich and idle gathered to take the cure and the casinos made their profits. And since the main amusement was eating and drinking, these were the places to which the most ambitious young chefs were drawn. Cuisine minceur—later to develop into nouvelle cuisine— were inventions of the innovative chefs who catered to the overindulged and overweight in the spa-hotels. It was here, during the school holidays, I added further strands of experience to Bernadette's lessons. The chefs catering to the new body-conscious clients, such as my grandmother, were all young, eager, and experimenting with new techniques, particularly the development of a new and lighter style of haute cuisine which appealed to the fashionable who were anxious to retain their figures.

When I married and had a family of my own, I added another level to my experience when I took us all (four children and husband) to live for one school year in the hinterland of Castelnaudary in the Languedoc—la France profonde, deepest France—so the children might have some experience of the French attitude to the good things of life. Living in an isolated farmhouse among a rural community whose way of life was still, in the seventies, as close to self-sufficiency as might be found anywhere in Europe, we had no choice but to follow the example of our neighbors and eat as the locals ate, acquiring along the way an understanding of peasant cookery—cuisine paysanne—the cooking of what comes to hand.

The great Curnonsky—gourmet, critic, boulevardier of the Belle Epoque, friend of Marcel Proust, author of the 32-volume *La France Gastronomique,* and acknowledged father of modern French gastronomy—defined three interlinked traditions as crucial to the identification of a national culinary habit. The first, he explained, is haute cuisine, the grand gastronomy of the court. The second, cuisine bourgeois, the cooking of the citizens of the towns who had access to all good things. The third—some would say the most valuable—is peasant cookery, the culinary habit of those who cook and eat what they grow, harvest and gather for themselves. Only by considering all three of these strands, he concluded, can the excellence of the national cuisine be measured. And France, he observed, excels in all three.

France, as an affiliation of kingdoms, duchies, and counties of relatively recent date (a mere five centuries or so), has always been resolutely regional. Beyond the obvious divisions (such as the region's preferred frying-medium: olive oil in the south, goose fat in the middle, butter in the north) a nation capable of appreciating five hundred different cheeses is scarcely likely to be willing to sacrifice diversity to mass-production, whether of ingredients or culinary habit. Allegiances are to locality—city, village, valley, community—and regional dishes reflect what is grown, gathered, or husbanded in the area, a culinary style known as cuisine du terroir, the cooking of the terrain. Visitors looking for French food in a French town, accustomed in their home-territory to a wide choice of culinary styles, are often startled when they find the same menu posted outside every restaurant of the region. The exceptions to this are cosmopolitan cities such as Paris—which, as the capital, had no need to develop a particular culinary style since everyone else's was readily available. Cuisine du terroir makes the choucroute of Alsace as different from the garbures of Gascogny as the pissaladière of Provence from the moules marinières of Brittany.

The French have never been squeamish about what they eat, still less about the form in which they buy it. Offal, both fresh and in the form of tripe-sausages, is eaten without inhibition. Feet and heads are left on poultry so that the purchaser can identify the breed as well as appreciate the freshness. Anyone who lives within reach of the sea expects to buy fish straight from the net: at least one boat of any inshore fleet sells its catch direct to the customers. In the fishmonger, the catch is displayed in the round—with scales, heads and innards still in place—and is prepared at the request of the purchaser. Shellfish and crustaceans are sold live in the confident expectation that the purchaser will know what to do with them.

If he or she wants something ready prepared, the French cook goes to the traiteur, the cooked-food shop, and cheerfully admits as much, recommending the place to friends. The traiteur, too, provides the little hors d'œuvres without which no French repast is worthy of the name: rillettes, olives, pâtés, charcuterie, the classic salads (potato, carrot, celery root). Desserts are rarely prepared at home; meals usually end with cheese and fruit. If something special is called for, the best pâtisserie in town is alerted and the dessert ordered in advance—shop-bought tarts have glamor, as does the Twelfth Night pithiviers or the Christmas bûche de noël. And then there's the crowning glory, the weekly visit to the cheese merchant for a slice of Roquefort, a slab of Cantal, a soft-hearted Camembert, a few little rounds of blue-bloomed goat's-milk cheese.

In France, all these good things are considered an indivisible part of the joy of life: of the French it can truly be said that they live to eat. Whether they do this in Michelin-starred restaurants (the natural heirs of court cuisine); or allow the traiteur to take most of the strain (one of the pleasures of the town-based bourgeoisie); or take the rural way and cook whatever's in season right now. In France, the produce of small-holding self-sufficiency, while no longer a matter of necessity, remains a choice, even for those who rely on others to bring it to market.

Of the thousands of recipes which have fair claim to inclusion in a book on the classic cooking of France, I have chosen nearer a hundred. The task was not easy. In the end it came down to a simple matter of personal choice. I have included those recipes that I consider essential to pass on to my own grandchildren, just as Bernadette passed hers on to me.

Bon appétit.

*hors d'œuvres*

# *tapenade*

## BLACK OLIVE *and* ANCHOVY PASTE

The tapenade, surprisingly, is a relatively new introduction to the hors d'œuvre repertoire. A restaurant invention from the Côte d'Azure, it takes its name from the capers—tapeno in the Provençale patois—that perfume the mix. Nevertheless, the idea of pitting and pounding olives to make a savory paste to eat with bread is nothing new, it's just the sophisticated blending with other storecupboard ingredients that makes the difference. For the basic olive paste, choose the wrinkled, ripe, chewy little frost-cured olives of Nyons or anywhere in Upper Provence.

Makes about 1lb

1½ cups black Provençal olives
6 preserved anchovy fillets
1 tablespoon preserved tuna
2 tablespoons preserved capers
1 teaspoon freshly milled black pepper
1 teaspoon dried thyme
about ½ cup olive oil
1 teaspoon brandy

1 Drain the olives and remove the stones. Drain the anchovy fillets. Salted anchovy fillets from a barrel have to be soaked in milk for 30 minutes and then boned.

2 Pound all the solid ingredients together to a fine paste in a mortar. Trickle in enough olive oil to make a smooth scoopable paste, beating with a wooden spoon as for a mayonnaise. Stir in the brandy. Alternatively, save your strength and puree the whole lot in a food processor.

3 To store the tapenade, pot it, cover with a tight-fitting lid, and keep in the fridge.

**SERVING SUGGESTION** ~ Serve with chunks of baguette and red radishes. In France, radishes are sold with their leaves, with the stalks bunched into a posy, and this is how they appear on the table.

**USING TAPENADE** ~ Tapenade can be used as a stuffing for hard-cooked eggs. Shell and halve the eggs lengthwise. Remove the yolks and mash with 1 teaspoon tapenade per yolk. Spoon or pipe the mixture back into the whites.

# brandade de morue

T his is the dish traditionally served in Provence and the
Languedoc at the souper maigre, the fasting supper of
Christmas Eve, at which neither meat, wine nor sweet things
can be served. You can buy morue salt cod pre-soaked and ready
to go; if not, choose a middle cut and soak it for 48 hours in
several changes of water.

❧

Serves 6–8

1lb salt cod, pre-soaked
1 onion, cut into chunks
2 bay leaves
2–3 fennel tops or 1 teaspoon fennel seeds
1 teaspoon white peppercorns
1 cups extra virgin olive oil, warmed to finger-heat
2–3 tablespoons cream, warmed
1 potato, boiled, mashed and still warm
(optional, but it helps the emulsion)
2–3 garlic cloves, crushed
1 black olive

TO SERVE
melba toast
(fine slices of dry bread toasted in the oven until crisp)

1 Cut the fish into 3–4 chunks and put these in a pan with the onion, bay leaves, fennel tops or seeds, and peppercorns. Cover with water and bring gently to the boil.

2 Remove the pan from the heat as soon as the water gives a good belch, and pour in a glassful of cold water. Leave to stand for 5 minutes. Then drain, skin, and flake the fish, discarding any bones.

3 Pound the flaked fish with the potato (if using), the garlic, and a little of the oil, and then mash thoroughly and vigorously. Beat in the rest of the oil gradually, as if making a mayonnaise, adding the cream towards the end. Beat the mixture to a thick, scoopable white puree. You can also do this in a food processor, but the result will be noticeably smoother and whiter than that achieved by hand-beating.

4 Pile the mixture into a bowl and top with a single black olive. Serve at room temperature with melba toast.

# rillettes

## POTTED PORK

Neither a pâté nor a paste, but something in between, you'll find this succulent preparation on sale in charcuteries and pork-butchers throughout France, prepared to a recipe scarcely changed since the days of Charlemagne. The lard which serves as the potting agent for the meat is either goose fat, made with the rich leavings from the foie-gras goose, or panne de porc, the soft white fat that surrounds a pig's kidney. Serve rillettes with fresh radishes, pickles, sweet butter, rough salt (preferably sel de Guerande) and chunks of fresh baguette or pain de campagne—country bread—the name given to a round loaf suitable for carrying in the pocket. Rillettes may also be served as part of a selection of charcuterie: jambon de bayonne, saucisson sec, and andouillette.

∽

Serves 8–10

1 cup goose fat or freshly made pork lard
3lb belly pork, skinned and cut into chunks
3 teaspoons salt
1 teaspoon freshly milled pepper
1 teaspoon ground allspice
a small bunch of thyme, rosemary and bay

1 Melt the lard gently in a heavy pan without letting it bubble. Add the pork and stir over a very low heat until the fat begins to run from the meat.

2 Add 1 tablespoon water, the salt, pepper, and allspice. Tuck in the herbs between the pieces of meat and cook very gently for 3 hours until the fat has completely melted and the meat is absolutely soft. Alternatively, bake in the coolest possible oven, at 167°F. Keep a careful watch for sticking, stirring the pork regularly. The fat should never bubble and the temperature must remain very low throughout cooking. At the end, there should be no water and the fat should be clear and the meat meltingly soft.

3 Remove the herbs. Skim off and save a ladleful of the surface fat for sealing the pots. Then using two forks, pull the meat apart, mixing it with the fat until well blended or pound it in a mortar (or use a food processor sparingly) to make a smoother mix. Taste and adjust the seasoning.

4 Pot the rillettes in small sterilized jars and leave to cool. Pour in a layer of the reserved melted fat to seal. The rillettes are ready immediately or will keep, undisturbed, for up to a month in the fridge or almost indefinitely in the freezer.

**PREPARING PORK LARD** ~ When preparing pork lard, take care to strip the little fat globules from the membranes and melt it very slowly with enough water to prevent it from browning.

# pâté de campagne

## COUNTRY PÂTÉ

A pâté, strictly speaking, is a pie, a description that indicates a pie crust; however, such refinements do not apply in the rural kitchen, where a jacket of finely sliced salt-cured belly pork—petit salé—or bacon serves to keep the mixture moist, the main purpose of the crust. You can replace the lean pork with the same volume of chicken or game, but do not omit the fat pork as wild meat needs something rich and fatty to balance its natural dryness.

**2lb boneless lean pork shoulder, cubed**
**8oz belly pork, skinned and cubed**
**1 tablespoon white brandy or Calvados (optional)**
**1 garlic clove, coarsely crushed**
**1 teaspoon dried thyme**
**1 teaspoon dried rosemary**
**1 teaspoon juniper berries, crushed**
**1 egg**
**scant ½ cup dry white wine**
**1 teaspoon ground allspice**
**1 teaspoon salt**
**1 teaspoon crushed black peppercorns**
**2 tablespoons fresh bread crumbs**
**about 10 thin slices salt-cured belly pork (petit salé) or fatty bacon**
**2–3 bay leaves**

~∞~

1  For a gamey flavor, start the day before and marinate the pork overnight: place both types in a dish with the brandy or Calvados (if using), garlic, thyme, rosemary, and juniper.

2  Preheat the oven to 350°F. Drain the meat reserving all the marinade. Chop half the pork shoulder and half the belly pork either using a sharp knife or briefly in a food processor. Mince the remainder. Place all the meat in a bowl.

3  Fork the egg with the wine and pour this over the meat. Add the reserved marinade, allspice, salt, and peppercorns. Work the ingredients well with the meat and mix in the bread crumbs.

4 Line a 1lb loaf pan with salt pork or bacon, leaving the ends overlapping the rim to fold over the top. Pack in the meat—the mixture should about two-thirds fill the pan. Top with the bay leaves and fold over the ends of the lining.

5 Cut a piece of foil large enough to cover the pan and pleat it down the middle to allow room for expansion. Cover the pan with this foil and set it in a bain-marie, a roasting pan into which you have poured enough boiling water to come half way up the sides of the loaf pan.

6 Bake for about 1 hour, until the pâté is perfectly firm and well-shrunk from the sides of the pan. Test with a skewer thrust deep into the middle: the juices should run clear. Leave to cool. Cover with a clean cloth and set a weighted board on top. Leave to rest and firm up overnight—this is important or the pâté will not hold together.

**SERVING SUGGESTION** ~ Serve with a bunch of little rosy radishes, black olives (or a tapenade, the more elegant alternative), and chunks of freshly baked baguette—a pâté without bread is unthinkable.

French pork-butchery, traditionally a specialist business reflecting the importance of the pig in the life of rural households, is an art as well as a craft. Pork-butchers take pride in preparing their own charcuterie, a definition applied to pork-products of a lightly preserved kind as well as the more durable (and familiar) air-cured hams and slicing-sausages. The repertoire evolved commercially to take care of the less saleable bits—innards and those parts which are too fatty or bony or troublesome to prepare—but was, in essence, a response to the need to add shelf-life to perishable foodstuffs in the days when refrigeration was not an option. Any self-respecting pork-butcher on market-day will be able to offer half a dozen freshly-cooked pâtés both rough and smooth; a choice of rillettes and rillons—shredded pork conserved in lard; petit salé—salt-cured belly pork—useful for enriching bean-dishes as well as, thinly sliced, for lining the pâté-tin or protecting the breast of a bird from the heat of the oven. There will, too, be trotters ready-cooked, boned, and breadcrumbed for grilling, head-cheese set in its own jelly, pork-knuckles, and bits to strengthen the pot-au-feu. For those who appreciate blood-puddings there'll be boudin noir as well as the creamy, more delicate boudin blanc; for those who love innards, there'll be the peppery tripe-sausages—andouille and andouillettes—tightly rolled into bolsters for grilling, delicious with strong French mustard. The French housewife takes pride in her choice of charcutier, values what he does, and wouldn't dream of pretending she'd made something herself if she hadn't. Being prepared to pay for the butcher's expertise is part of the pleasure.

# pâté de foie de porc

## PORK LIVER PÂTÉ

This is an honest country recipe for ensuring that the more perishable products of the rural household's annual pig-slaughter did not go to waste—a responsibility now transferred to the pork-butcher.

∾

### Serves 4–6

1 tablespoon pork lard or butter
1lb pork liver, cut into strips
2 shallots or 1 small onion, finely chopped
8oz lean pork shoulder
8oz belly pork
1 egg
1 teaspoon dried thyme
½ teaspoon juniper berries, crushed
½ teaspoon grated nutmeg
¼ teaspoon ground cloves
salt and freshly milled pepper
8–10 thin slices salt-cured belly pork (petit salé) or fatty bacon
2 bay leaves

TO SERVE
radishes/pickled gherkins
baguette/sweet butter

1 Melt the butter or lard in a skillet. Add the liver and onion and turn the ingredients in the butter until the meat stiffens, but is still pink. Remove from the heat.

2 Preheat the oven to 350°F. Mince the shoulder and belly pork together. Chop or mince the contents of the pan with the minced pork. Transfer to a bowl. Using your hands, work in the egg, thyme, juniper, nutmeg, and cloves. Season with salt and pepper.

3 Line a 1lb loaf pan with slices of salt pork or bacon, reserving some for the top. Pack in the meat mixture. Place the bay leaves on top and cover with bacon slices. Set the pan in a bain-marie, a roasting pan into which you have poured enough boiling water to come half way up the sides of the loaf pan.

4 Bake for about 1 hour, until the top browns a little. Cover with foil and continue baking for another 30 minutes, until the juices run clear when a skewer is pushed into the middle.

5 Place a weight on top of the pâté and leave it to cool, preferably overnight. The pâté will keep for 2 weeks in the fridge.

6 Serve thickly sliced, with radishes, pickled gherkins, fresh baguette, and sweet butter.

# *confit de foie gras*

## POTTED GOOSE LIVER

The goose and the duck are both candidates for engorgeage, a process by which the birds are force fed until their livers are very enlarged and full of fat. Maize is the usual fodder, chestnuts and walnuts traditional. This condition is not entirely unnatural as it was recorded in Egypt during the time of the Pharoahs, when the livers of migrant geese that had stuffed themselves on the young grasses on the flood plain of the Nile were so swollen they prevented the birds from becoming airborn. Toulouse, Périgueux, and Strasbourg are the main centres of foie-gras production in France. In truffle-producing areas, such as the Périgord, slivers of the fresh tuber—in season at the same time as the goose—are included.

Serves 8–10

1 fresh foie gras weighing 2–3lb
1–2 tablespoons coarse salt
1 tablespoon Armagnac or white brandy (optional)
1 fresh black Périgord truffle, brushed and
cut into slivers (optional)
1½ cups pure white goose or duck fat
pain de levain (country sour-dough bread) to serve

1 Remove any veins from the foie gras. Check the thick end of each lobe for the main vein; once found, tug it gently to expose its full length as well as the subsidiary veins, and remove them carefully with a small sharp knife. Remove any dark blood vessels. Do not worry about making a mess of the liver as it will re-form as it cooks. Place the liver on a clean china plate and sprinkle it all over with the salt and the Armagnac or brandy (if using). Cover with another clean plate and weight it down. Leave overnight to drain.

2 Preheat the oven to 375°F. Drain off the juices, dust off excess salt, and pat the liver dry. If using truffle, make little slits in the liver and push the truffle slivers into them. Weigh the liver and calculate the cooking time at 20 minutes per 1lb. Pack the liver into a terrine that will just accommodate it. Ladle in enough melted goose fat to submerge the liver completely.

3 Cover with foil, shiny side down, and transfer to a bain-marie, a roasting pan into which you have poured enough boiling water to come half way up the sides of the terrine. Bake for the calculated time, until the juices run clear but are still pale pink when the liver is pierced with a sharp skewer. Allow to cool. Serve country-style with toasted sour-dough bread, pain de levain.

**SELECTING FOIE GRAS** ~ To choose foie, look for firmness and paleness—ivory lightly tinged with pink (Strasbourg foie is naturally pinker). A yellow tint is a sign, along with excessive size, that the liver will be overly fatty. There should also be no sign of green staining, an indication of a punctured gall bladder which, if allowed to seep into the liver, turns the whole liver bitter.

# escargots à la bourguignonne

## VINEYARD SNAILS *with* GARLIC BUTTER

All snails, of whatever size or breed, are edible. Our ancestors loved them: stone-age middens are full of the debris of snail-feasts. The only danger lies not in the meat itself, but in what the creature might have ingested. Its digestive system is capable of processing the most toxic substances and depositing them in the cloaca, the little dark curl of intestine at the end of the body. Toxicity can be removed either by a period of starvation or hibernation, or control of the diet by other means (migrating the snails to the vineyard), or by removing the meat from the shell and pinching off the cloaca after a short (5 minute) plunge in the boiling pot. After this, a gentle simmer with aromatics and wine will improve the flavor while tenderizing the meat; this preliminary will have been carried out if you buy snails ready-prepared for finishing. In France two varieties are eaten. The smaller of the two is the petit gris, a snail with a soft gray body and a brown shell marked with a feathery pattern; the other is the larger Burgundy, or vineyard, snail. Both are endangered in the wild and are largely replaced with imported snails from Turkey and the Far East. For this dish, you need the larger snails. Allow 6–12 ready prepared snails with their shells per person.

Serves 4–8

**48 ready-prepared snails with shells**
**2–3 tablespoons Pernod (optional)**

GARLIC BUTTER
**2¼ sticks sweet butter, softened**
**2 garlic cloves, crushed**
**1 tablespoon finely chopped shallot**
**2 tablespoons finely chopped flat-leaf parsley**
**salt and freshly milled pepper**

TO SERVE
**fresh baguette**

1 Preheat the oven to 350°F. Arrange the empty snail shells, mouths pointing upwards, in special snail platters or in a roasting pan on a bed of rough salt (dishwasher salt is fine). Pop a drop of Pernod (if using) into each shell.

2 Mash the ingredients for the garlic butter together until well blended, seasoning with a little salt and plenty of freshly milled pepper. Drop a little butter into the base of a shell, top with the snail meat, and close the shell with another knob of butter. Replace the shell in the container, mouth still pointing upwards. Continue until all are filled.

3 Bake the snails for 20–30 minutes, until steaming hot and bubbling. Serve with chunks of fresh baguette for mopping up the butter.

# cassolette d'escargots

SNAIL CASSEROLE

This is a sophisticated Provençal recipe for France's mighty mollusks. Snails in garlic butter is all very well in dairy-country, but in the land of the olive tree where dairy foods are traditionally absent, oil is the enrichment of choice.

❧

Serves 6

2 glasses white wine
1lb shelled cooked snails (cooking broth reserved, if possible)
2 tablespoons olive oil
1 tablespoon all-purpose flour
2 tablespoons grated cheese, such as Cantal or Gruyère
salt and freshly milled pepper
pinch of sugar (optional)
2–3 sage leaves, finely chopped
2 tablespoons chopped parsley
2 tablespoons snipped chives

TO FINISH
2 heaped tablespoons fresh bread crumbs
2 tablespoons chopped parsley
1 garlic clove, finely chopped
2 tablespoons grated cheese
1 tablespoon olive oil

1 Bring the wine to the boil in a pan with a ladleful of the snail broth (see page 30) or any decent stock, and cook until the liquid is reduced by half.

2 Work the oil with the flour to a paste, then whisk it into the reduced broth. Simmer until thick enough to coat the back of a wooden spoon. Stir in the grated cheese. Taste and add salt and pepper—maybe a pinch of sugar if the wine was a little tart.

3 Add the snails and simmer gently for 10 minutes to marry the flavors. Stir in the chopped herbs.

4 To finish, preheat the broiler. Spread the snails in a gratin dish. Toss the bread crumbs with the parsley, garlic, and grated cheese, and sprinkle over the snails. Drizzle with the olive oil and flash under the broiler to gild the top. If the snails are prepared in advance ready for finishing, preheat the oven to 350°F and bake for 15 minutes to bubble and brown.

# cuisses de grenouille à l'ail

## FROGS' LEGS *with* GARLIC AND PARSLEY

Frogs' legs were readily available from the wild some thirty years ago, when my children attended school in Castelnaudary in the Languedoc. We lived in a farmhouse surrounded by fields, copses, and ponds where frogs could be caught by attaching a scrap of red rag to a fishing line. Frogs can no longer be legally caught in the wild and France's supplies of muscular little frogs' legs—they always come in pairs—are mostly imported from the paddy fields of South East Asia. Possible substitutes are quails' legs—once cooked they look much the same (sauté the breasts with mushrooms).

Serves 4–6

**8–12 pairs frogs' legs**
**1–2 tablespoons all-purpose flour, seasoned**
**4 tablespoons olive oil**
**½ stick sweet butter**
**4 garlic cloves, finely chopped**
**2 tablespoons chopped parsley**
**squeeze of lemon juice**

TO SERVE
**quartered lemons**
**fresh baguette**

❧

1 Dust the frogs' legs lightly with the seasoned flour.

2 Heat the oil in a heavy skillet. Add the butter and wait until it froths. Lower the heat a little, lay the frogs' legs gently in the pan and sauté for 2–3 minutes on each side, until they take a little color and the meat feels firm when pressed with your thumb.

3 Transfer to a warm serving dish. Add the garlic to the pan drippings and fry for a couple of minutes until the garlic softens, then stir in the parsley and add a squeeze of lemon.

4 Return the frogs' legs to the pan and reheat gently. Serve with quartered lemons and chunks of very fresh baguette.

# galantine de gibier

## GAME TERRINE *with* JELLY

You never can tell what the hunters will bring home. A galantine—the French method of potting by slow cooking with aromatics in just enough water to cover the meats—is the practical way to deal with a mixed bag of furred and feathered beasts of uncertain age and toughness. If you lack a good proportion of bone to meat, include a well-scrubbed pig's trotter or a piece of veal shin to help the juices set to a firm jelly. This popular dish is sold sliced by weight from the traiteur, the cooked-food shop. It is good with a few salt-pickled caper buds and baby gherkins (cornichons) to cut the richness, or serve it with a salad and new potatoes as a light supper.

❦

Serves 8–10

**4–6lb wild boar or any game on the bone, chopped into manageable chunks or portions**

**2–3 thyme sprigs**

**2–3 bay leaves**

**1 tablespoon juniper berries, crushed**

**1 tablespoon salt**

**1 teaspoon crushed black peppercorns**

**1 tablespoon Calvados or white brandy**

**4–5 thin slices bayonne ham**

1 Preheat the oven to 325°F. Pack the meat, bones and all, into a large casserole or stone crock with the thyme, bay leaves, juniper berries, salt, and peppercorns. Pour in the Calvados or brandy and enough water to cover the meat.

2 Cover with a lid that fits very tightly. (Seal the rim with a flour-and-water paste if the lid does not fit really snugly.) Cook for 3–4 hours, until the meat is really soft.

3 Remove the meat and strain the broth. While the meat is still warm, strip it off the bones, and dice it. The broth needs to be really strong if it is to set properly in a jelly: boil it until it is reduced to about scant 2 cups.

4 Line a 2 lb loaf pan with the ham, leaving generous flaps overhanging the rim. Pack in the meat mixture, filling the pan right to the top. Pour in enough of the concentrated stock to wet the meat thoroughly. Fold the loose flaps of ham over the top, cover with foil, and weight down. Leave the pan in a cool place overnight for the jelly to set. To serve, use a knife dipped in boiling water to cut the meat in slices.

**STORING THE GALANTINE** ~ The galantine keeps well in the fridge, but it does not freeze. The jelly will separate and there'll be no hope for the galantine, other than to boil it again and bake it in a pie.

# terrine de legumes

## VEGETABLE TERRINE

This is a useful starter for vegetarians as the French hors d'œuvre table tends to be meat orientated. The choice of vegetables is up to you, though these look particularly pretty and the flavors are well balanced.

∽

Serves 6–8

1lb spinach or broccoli
1lb celery root or cauliflower
1lb carrots or swede
3 large eggs
1 cup light cream
¼ teaspoon freshly grated nutmeg
salt and freshly milled pepper

1 If using spinach, wash it and then place in a lidded pan with the water that clings to the leaves. Cook briefly until wilted and drain thoroughly, squeezing out the water by hand. Cut the other vegetables into bite-sized pieces and cook each type separately in boiling salted water until soft. Drain thoroughly, and puree the vegetables, still keeping them separate.

2 Preheat the oven to 300°F. Butter a 1lb loaf pan. Separate the eggs. Mix the yolks thoroughly into the cream. Whisk the whites until fluffy—smooth and light. Mix a third of the yolk and cream mixture into each vegetable puree. Season carefully before folding in the whites, equally divided among the three mixtures.

3 Spread the purees in layers in the prepared pan, first spinach, then celery root, then carrot. Cover with foil, shiny side down, and set the tin in a bain-marie, a roasting pan into which you have poured enough boiling water to come half way up the sides of the loaf pan. Bake for 1½ hours, until perfectly set—test by pressing with your finger. Allow to cool and become firm.

4 When you are ready to serve the terrine, unmould it on to a plate. Serve at room temperature, cut into beautiful three-coloured slices.

**SERVING TIP** ~ The terrine is good with a chilled sauce, maybe créme fraîche blended with finely chopped watercress or chives, or a fresh tomato coulis (see page 255).

# pissaladière

## PROVENÇALE ONION TART

This specialty of the bakers of Nice is a close relation of the Italian pizza—some might say the original of the genre, since it gets its name from the pissalat niçoise, a paste made by pounding salt-cured anchovies with olive oil, thyme, pepper, and bay. In its simplest form, the base is a thin bread dough topped by a thick layer of softly-fried onion.

Serves 6–8

2 cups all-purpose flour
½ teaspoon salt
3 tablespoons olive oil
1 egg
½ teaspoon finely grated lemon zest

### TOPPING
2lb onions, thinly sliced
1–2 tablespoons olive oil
2–3 garlic cloves, finely chopped
6–8 anchovy fillets
2 tablespoons black olives
2 tablespoons salt-cured capers, rinsed and drained
1 tablespoon chopped fresh thyme

1 Work the flour, salt, olive oil, egg, and lemon zest together by hand, adding about 4 tablespoons warm water to form a soft, smooth ball of dough that leaves the sides of the bowl clean. (Alternatively, this may be done in a food processor.) Flatten the dough a little, cover it with plastic wrap and set it aside to rest for 30 minutes.

2 Meanwhile, prepare the filling. Fry the onions gently in the oil until they soften and gild—don't hurry the process or let them burn.

3 Preheat the oven to 425°F. Transfer the dough to a floured surface and roll it out to fit a large baking tray, about 10in square. Spread the dough with the onions and top with the garlic, anchovies, olives, capers, and thyme.

4 Bake for 20–25 minutes, until the pastry is crisp and golden, and the edges have blistered brown.

# salade niçoise

## SALAD NIÇOISE

*A* *robust, chunky summer salad, this is served as a first
course or a light lunch. Named after Nice, where the
Italian culinary influence is strong, the flavoring herb is basil.
Do not include cooked vegetables as the flavors should be fresh,
bright, and clean to contrast with the salty, fermented flavor of
the preserved fish.*

Serves 4

4 hard-cooked eggs
1lb ripe tomatoes
1 small English cucumber
1 romaine lettuce heart, roughly chopped
6 salted anchovies or anchovies canned in oil
5oz salted tuna in oil
1 garlic clove
6 tablespoons olive oil
2 tablespoons wine vinegar
1 green bell pepper, seeded and sliced into rings
4–5 scallions, chopped
1 mild purple onion, cut vertically into thin slivers
handful of shelled young fava beans or baby green beans (raw)
1 tablespoon black olives
about 12 fresh basil leaves, roughly torn

1 Peel the eggs and quarter them neatly. Chop the tomatoes and cucumber into bite-sized chunks. Tear the lettuce into bite-sized pieces. Drain the anchovies and the tuna. Break the tuna into large flakes and separate the anchovies into fillets.

2 Rub the salad bowl with the cut clove of garlic. Pour the oil and vinegar into the bowl and use a fork to mix them. Toss the lettuce, tomatoes, cucumber, green pepper, scallions, purple onion, and beans with the oil and vinegar. Do not add salt – the fish and olives provide quite enough of their own.

3 Finish with the olives, basil leaves, eggs, tuna, and anchovies.

**HARD-COOKED EGGS** ~ Bring the eggs to room temperature. Place them in enough cold water to cover them completely and bring the water to the boil. After 3 minutes, remove the pan from the heat and leave the eggs to stand for 8–10 minutes, depending on their size. Plunge the eggs into cold water to loosen the shells, then peel them.

**PREPARING SALTED ANCHOVIES** ~ Salted anchovies from the barrel need to be soaked in milk for a few hours to make them less salty. Then they should be drained and de-whiskered by removing the hairy little bones—pinch them between the thumb and forefinger to loosen, then pull them out.

# *salade de pommes de terre*

### POTATO SALAD

*C*hoose one of the small, almond-shaped potato varieties
that remain firm after cooking, such as Charlotte or La
Ratte, France's salad potato of choice. Although the marjoram
included in this recipe is not essential, it has a warm earthy
fragrance that gives it a particular affinity with potato.

Serves 4–6

**2lb small new potatoes, scrubbed**
**4 tablespoons olive oil**
**1–2 slices day-old bread, cut into cubes**
**1 garlic clove, crushed with a pinch of salt**

DRESSING
**2 tablespoons mild mustard (preferably Dijon mustard)**
**2 tablespoons wine vinegar**
**1 glass white wine or meat stock**
**4 tablespoons olive oil**
**salt and freshly milled pepper**

TO FINISH
**1 tablespoon capers, drained**
**1 tablespoon small black olives**
**small bunch of scallions, trimmed and chopped**
**a few marjoram leaves to finish**

1 Cook the potatoes in plenty of well-salted boiling water for 15–20 minutes, until perfectly tender. Drain immediately, then return the potatoes to the heat for a moment to dry them off.

2 Meanwhile, heat the oil in a skillet. As soon as it smokes—a blue haze, nothing more—drop in the bread cubes and fry them until crisp and golden. Remove, toss with the crushed garlic, and reserve.

3 Set the skillet with its oily drippings back on the heat and stir in the mustard, vinegar, and wine or stock. Bubble up for a moment and whisk in the oil and seasoning. If you're lucky, the dressing will form an emulsion; if not, no matter. Tip the dressing into the bowl in which you mean to serve the salad.

4 Slice the potatoes into the bowl, skin, and all, and turn them in the hot liquid. Add the capers, olives, and scallions and turn them with the potatoes. The potatoes will drink it all up as they cool. Finish, when cool, with a few leaves of marjoram.

**VARIATIONS** ~ Other ingredients can be added to the potato salad. Possible inclusions are diced cucumber, hard-cooked egg, tomato, diced apple, walnuts, toasted pine kernels, preserved tuna or anchovies.

# ratatouille

## PROVENÇAL VEGETABLES IN OLIVE OIL

*T*his is a dish for high summer when the sunny vegetables
of Provence are at peak perfection. The eggplant should
be cut into dice about the size of a hazelnut (modern varieties
do not need salting); the zucchini should be quartered if large
and cut into slices as thick as your little finger. Each element of
the assembly is permitted to take the heat separately and
combined at the end—a little labor intensive but essential if the
dish is to be as good as it should be.

Serves 6

⅔ cup olive oil (possibly more)
2 eggplant, diced
2 red bell peppers, seeded and thinly sliced
1 green chili pepper, seeded and chopped (optional but good)
3–4 small zucchini, sliced
2–3 onions, finely sliced
4–5 garlic cloves
3–4 ripe plum tomatoes, peeled and diced
(bottled or canned are fine)
1½ teaspoons dried rosemary
1½ teaspoons dried thyme
salt and freshly milled pepper

1 Heat half the oil in a roomy skillet. Add the eggplant, sprinkle with a little salt, and fry gently until perfectly tender and lightly caramelized. The eggplant will first fry, then soak up the oil, and finally give it back and fry again.

2 Transfer the eggplant to a large sieve set over a bowl to catch the drippings. Reheat the pan with another 2 tablespoons oil and add the red peppers and the chili (if using). Fry gently until the peppers are soft and lightly caramelized, then transfer them to the sieve.

3 Reheat the pan with another 2 tablespoons oil and fry the zucchini until soft and lightly gilded, then transfer to the sieve with the eggplant.

4 Return the drippings from the vegetables to the pan and fry the onions and garlic until soft and golden. Remove and drain in the sieve over the bowl. Reheat the pan with the remaining oil and any residual drippings and fry the tomatoes gently until soft and collapsed.

5 Stir in the rosemary and thyme, and the vegetables from the sieve. Season with salt and pepper, and bubble gently for 5–10 minutes to marry the flavors. Serve at room temperature.

**NOTE** ~ The only essential ingredients are the eggplant, garlic, onions, and oil.

# celeri-rave en rémoulade

GRATED CELERY ROOT *with* MUSTARD VINAIGRETTE

A rémoulade is simply a mustard-thickened vinaigrette which often includes capers, chopped scallion, hard-cooked egg, and chopped herbs, and is used as a sharp little sauce for cold meats from the charcuterie. Here it is used as a dressing for grated raw celery root. Lighter and sharper than a mayonnaise-dressed salad, celery root salad can be bought ready-made in the traiteur by weight, where it is sold as one-third of a classic trio of salads. The other two salads are finely-grated raw carrot dressed with lemon juice, olive oil, and black olives, and baked beetroot dressed with olive oil, garlic, and parsley.

Serves 4

**1 celery root**
**1 tablespoon mild Dijon mustard**
**6 tablespoons olive oil**
**1 tablespoon wine vinegar or cider vinegar**
**salt and freshly milled black pepper**
**chopped flat-leaf parsley (optional) to garnish**

1 Peel the celery root, cut it into manageable chunks, and grate it coarsely. (Use a food processor for this if you have the appropriate attachment.)

2 Add the celery root to a large pan of boiling salted water and bring the water back to the boil—this should take about 3 minutes, just long enough to blanch the celery root. Transfer the celery root to a sieve or colander, pass it under the cold tap to stop the cooking process, and drain thoroughly.

3 To make the rémoulade: in a small bowl, work the mustard with the oil, whisking or forking the oil in drop by drop, as if making a mayonnaise. Add the vinegar as the sauce emulsifies. Taste and add salt and pepper.

4 Dress the celery root with the rémoulade. Finish with a handful of parsley—or not, as you please.

# asperges à la vinaigrette

## ASPARAGUS *with* OIL AND VINEGAR

The French like blanched asparagus—fat and white with a cream-colored tip—while the Germans like theirs blanched and tipped with violet, and the English (as well as the Spaniards) prefer theirs green. For the spears to remain perfectly blanched, they must be picked before dawn from beds well-heaped with sandy soil, so the tips which thrust upwards overnight have no chance to reach the light. The asparagus beds of southern France were planted as a replacement crop for the olive trees lost to the frost during the terrible winter of 1956. Although most of the crop is exported to northern markets, the locals appreciate theirs with no other sauce but the mild golden olive oil of Provence forked until blended with just enough vinegar to give it an edge.

∽

Serves 4

**2lb large white asparagus**
**½ cup extra virgin olive oil**
**2 tablespoons wine vinegar**
**salt and freshly milled black pepper**
**fresh baguette**

1 Have ready an asparagus steamer or a pan deep enough to accommodate the bundles of asparagus vertically; that is, with their heads in the air and the stalks in water. (You can improvise a steamer by cutting off the top of an empty 5-litre olive oil can.)

2 Wash and trim the asparagus stalks and tie them into neat bundles. Bring a large pan of salted water to a rolling boil and lower the bundles in, feet first. Prop them up so that the stalks are submerged but the tips are in steam only. Bring the water back to the boil, turn the heat down, and boil gently for 15–20 minutes, until the stalks are soft.

3 Meanwhile, prepare a pitcher of the olive oil forked up with the wine vinegar—leave the fork in the pitcher so that oil and vinegar can be blended again.

4 Lift the bundles of asparagus out of the pan, drain them thoroughly, and untie them. Serve the asparagus piping hot on a white napkin. Set out the pitcher of vinaigrette, a dish of rough salt, a pepper mill and bread for mopping. That's all.

**SERVING SUGGESTIONS FOR ASPARAGUS** ~ If you would rather serve the asparagus cold, accompany it with mayonnaise (see page 163). France's northerners—those who live in dairy country—prefer their asparagus served hot and sauced with melted butter or hollandaise sauce (see page 248).

# cèpes à la bordelaise

## SAUTÉED CEPS

**B**oletus edulis, most prized of the many varieties of edible wild fungi gathered throughout the woods and forests of Europe, are known in France as cèpes or bolets, in Italy as porcini, in Britain and America as penny buns or boletus. Large, meaty, firm-fleshed fungi, the edible members of the family are distinguished by their brown caps and spongy yellow underparts. A single cep can weigh half a kilo, though they weigh heavier if gathered on a wet day. They are gathered in the woods and forests of the northern hemisphere from mid-July until the first frosts of winter. The inhabitants of Bordeaux value them particularly highly and cook them in olive oil with garlic or shallots and parsley.

∽

Serves 4

**about 1lb ceps (at least 1 large cep per person)**
**4–5 tablespoons olive oil**
**salt and freshly milled pepper**
**4 tablespoons chopped flat-leaf parsley**
**2 garlic cloves or shallots, finely chopped**
**about 2 tablespoons fresh bread crumbs**

1 Ceps are magnets for creepy-crawlies, so inspect the fungi and remove any unwelcome interlopers. Trim the stalks sparingly, scraping off any moss and earth. Wipe the caps but do not rinse them unless they really need it. If your specimens are overly mature and dark, or were picked on a damp day, remove the spongy underparts. Slice.

2 Heat the oil in a roomy skillet. When the oil is hot but not smoking, put in the prepared ceps and sprinkle with a little salt to start the juices running. Fry for 5 minutes or so, until the edges of the slices begin to sizzle and brown—the time this takes depends on how wet the fungi were to begin with.

3 Add the garlic and parsley, and allow all to cook together gently for another 5 minutes. Stir in enough bread crumbs to absorb all the juices. Turn the heat up for a moment to gild the bread crumbs. That's all.

# champignons à la grecque

## MARINATED MUSHROOMS

A little salad of button mushrooms dressed with lemon juice and olive oil—this is modest but good. The cultivated mushroom, a descendent of *Agaricus campestris*, the common field mushroom, is known in France as *champignon de Paris* since it was commercially produced on the disused racecourses of Paris, abandoned in the aftermath of the Revolution.

Serves 4

**1lb very fresh button mushrooms**
**⅔ cup white wine**
**2 tablespoons olive oil**
**1 tablespoon lemon juice**
**1 teaspoon coriander seeds**
**pinch of dried thyme**
**1–2 bay leaves, crumbled**

TO FINISH
**1 tablespoon chopped parsley**

1 Wipe the mushrooms, slice finely, and spread them out in a suitable shallow dish.

2 Bring the remaining ingredients to the boil in a small pan and bubble up for 1–2 minutes, until the steam no longer smells of raw alcohol. Tip the contents of the pan over the mushrooms and leave to marinate overnight. Finish with parsley.

**NOTE** ~ To vary the flavor and add color, finish with 2–3 tablespoons chopped, peeled, and seeded tomato.

# croustade aux chanterelles

## CHANTERELLE TART

A recipe from Provence, for which the tart base is made with an olive oil pastry. Any wild or cultivated fungi can be substituted for the chanterelles, a late summer crop found under beech trees and in and around birch woods: look for their bright orange frills tucked under the leaf mould. Later in the autumn, choose a mixture of pied-de-mouton (hedgehog fungi), cèpe (boletus) and trompette de la mort (horn of plenty).

❧

Serves 4 as an appetizer

**8 cups all-purpose flour**
**4 tablespoons olive oil**
**½ teaspoon salt**

### FILLING
**2 tablespoons olive oil**
**5 cups sliced chanterelles or button mushrooms**
**1 large onion, finely sliced**
**1 thyme sprig**
**2 tablespoons chopped black olives**
**4 eggs**
**½ cup fresh goat's cheese**
**salt and freshly milled pepper**

1 Work the flour, olive oil, and salt for the pastry together vigorously with the hook of your hand, adding enough warm water to form a smooth ball which comes away from the sides of the mixing bowl. Flatten the ball of dough a little, cover with plastic wrap and set it to rest for 30 minutes, while you prepare the filling.

2 For the filling, heat the oil gently in a skillet, add the chanterelles, onion, and thyme and fry gently until the fungi yield their juice and begin to sizzle. When they all begin to brown a little, stir in the olives. Remove the pan from the heat, pick out the thyme, and let cool.

3 Preheat the oven to 400°F. Roll out the pastry to fit a 10in round tart pan. Prick the base and bake for 10–15 minutes, until the pastry is set. If the pastry bubbles, prick it again to release the air.

4 Meanwhile, beat the eggs with the soft goat's cheese, plenty of black pepper, and a little salt. Stir in the fungi mixture. Spread this filling in the tart case. Reduce the oven to 350°F and bake the tart for 35–40 minutes, until the filling is almost set but still a little trembly in the middle.

# morilles à la crème

## MOREL MUSHROOMS *with* CREAM

The morel, *Morcella esculenta*, is a spring mushroom, a lover not of woodland but of open spaces, found in rough pasture and on roadside verges. I have often found it in association with ground orchids, a species which likes the same habitat. The morel has a distinctive wrinkled cap and a fragrance almost as seductive as the truffle. It dries well without losing texture and flavor and in a sauce or stew dried is actually superior to fresh—1oz dried is equivalent to 5oz fresh.

Serves 4

**12oz fresh morels**
**½ stick sweet butter**
**salt and freshly milled pepper**
**1 tablespoon chopped parsley**
**pinch of dried thyme**
**½ cup crème fraîche**
**4 thick slices pain de campagne or robust country bread,**
**such as sour-dough bread**

1 Shake out any grit from the morels, slice off the woody ends of the stalks, and slice the little honeycombed caps.

2 Heat a little knob of butter in a small pan, add the fungi, and fry for 2–3 minutes, until their juices begin to run. Sprinkle with a little salt, the parsley, and a pinch of thyme, and fry until the fungi sizzle and brown a little. Stir in the crème fraîche, season with pepper, and bubble up for another couple of minutes.

3 Meanwhile, toast 4 slices of the bread. Pile the cream-sauced morels on the toast and finish with another turn of the pepper mill.

**NOTE** ~ Failing fresh morels (available at good delis or specialist greengrocers), substitute a few dried morels, pre-soaked in a little water and combined with oyster mushrooms.

# topinambours à la provençale

JERUSALEM ARTICHOKES *with* GARLIC AND OLIVES

The Jerusalem or root artichoke is a New World member of the daisy family, a group that includes the merry sunflower. The Italian for sunflower is girasole, hence "Jerusalem." The sweetness in the flesh is inulin, a natural sugar which can be eaten by diabetics. Their knobbly shape make Jerusalem artichokes tricky to peel: boil them in salted water for 10 minutes, then rub off the papery skin.

Serves 4

**1lb Jerusalem artichokes, peeled**
**2 tablespoons olive oil**
**1 tablespoon black olives, pitted or not, as preferred**
**2 tablespoons lemon juice**
**1 teaspoon finely grated lemon zest**
**⅛ cup white wine**
**about ⅔ cup chicken or vegetable stock**
**¼ teaspoon freshly grated nutmeg**
**freshly milled pepper**
**2 tablespoons chopped parsley**
**1 garlic clove, chopped**

1 Cut the artichokes into walnut-sized pieces, rinse, and transfer to a casserole or pan. Add the olive oil, olives, lemon juice and zest, wine, and enough stock to barely cover the pieces. Season with nutmeg and pepper—no salt yet.

2 Bring to the boil, turn down the heat, cover, and cook the artichokes until tender—25–30 minutes. Take the lid off and let any liquid boil away, so that the artichokes fry a little.

3 Stir in the garlic and parsley and bubble-fry for another minute. Taste and add salt if needed—unlikely, as the olives are quite salty enough. Serve at room temperature.

# artichauts à la barigoule

## ARTICHOKES COOKED LIKE TRUFFLES

Throughout the summer in Provençal markets, artichokes are sold on their stalks in great bunches for little more than the price of a cabbage, allowing cooks to be as profligate as they please. Better still, for a little extra, the hearts can be bought ready prepared. The aromatic cooking broth in this recipe is designed to give the artichokes the flavor of the barigoule, a pale-fleshed summer truffle.

Serves 4–6

8–12 artichoke hearts plus the upper stalks<br/>
4 tablespoons olive oil<br/>
1 large onion, finely chopped<br/>
2–3 garlic cloves, finely chopped<br/>
1 carrot, finely chopped<br/>
1–2 celery sticks, finely chopped<br/>
3 tablespoons finely chopped black olives<br/>
2 tablespoons chopped jambon cru (raw cured ham)<br/>
or lean bacon<br/>
1–2 dried or fresh thyme sprigs, crumbled or chopped<br/>
2 dried or fresh sage leaves, crumbled or chopped<br/>
1–2 bay leaves<br/>
1 glass white wine<br/>
salt and freshly milled pepper<br/>
a little sugar

TO FINISH<br/>
1 tablespoon chopped parsley<br/>
2–3 tablespoons fresh bread crumbs

1 Quarter the prepared artichoke hearts (see page 64). Trim and scrape the stalks to remove the inedible stringy outer layer and chop the tender centre into short bean-sized lengths.

2 Heat the olive oil in a heavy pan or flameproof casserole. Add the onion and garlic and fry gently until they take a little color. Add the carrot, celery, olives, ham or bacon, and herbs, and fry for a few minutes more.

3 Pour in the wine and a glass of water and bubble up. Stir in the artichoke pieces—hearts and stalks—and bubble up again. Turn down the heat, season with salt, pepper, and a little sugar, and cover loosely. Leave to simmer for 30–40 minutes until the artichokes are perfectly tender. Alternatively, preheat the oven to 350°F, cover the casserole (with foil if necessary), and cook in the oven for 45 minutes.

4 Check during cooking in case the vegetables need a little more water. By the end, the liquid should have reduced to an aromatic few tablespoons. If there is too much liquid, bubble it up fiercely to evaporate the excess. Stir in the parsley and enough bread crumbs to take up all the juice. Serve at room temperature.

**TO PREPARE AN ARTICHOKE HEART** ~ Have ready a bowl of cold water and squeeze in the juice of ½ lemon. Rinse the artichoke and trim off the stalk close to the base. Scrape the stalk to remove the hard exterior fibres, leaving the tender centre, and drop it into the lemon water so it does not discolor.

Snap off the tough outer leaves, then, with a sharp knife, cut off the tops of the remaining leaves within ½in of the base. Nick out the inner leaves, exposing the hairy choke. Remove the choke, scraping it out with a sharp spoon, and drop the prepared base into the water. The artichoke heart is now ready for cooking.

∽

## ALL ABOUT ARTICHOKES

The artichoke, a member of the thistle family native to the shores of the Mediterranean, produces a chemical, cynarin, which has the effect of making anything which is drunk afterwards taste sweeter—a disadvantage for wine-drinkers but pleasant for those who drink water. So noticeable is this effect that the plant acquired a bad reputation in Caesar's Rome, where the naturalist Pliny complained of its evil effects. The plant is also one of several capable of turning milk into curds for cheese-making, providing a replacement for animal rennet, a digestive organism found in the stomachs of all lactating mammals, including—lest we give ourselves airs above our station—ourselves. Take advantage of the association by serving plain-boiled artichokes with a little sauce of fresh cream cheese, well-seasoned and flavored with herbs, to spoon into the choke when you've eaten the tender bases of the leaves dipped in a vinaigrette. Allow 20–30 minutes in boiling salted water, depending on the size of artichokes, and when you're ready to eat the heart, don't forget to lift out the hairy little choke with a sharp knife. To prepare the cream cheese, beat 8oz fresh curd cheese with half its own volume of crème fraîche, season with salt and freshly milled black pepper, and beat in a finely chopped garlic clove and a tablespoon each of chopped parsley, chives, and chervil.

# soufflé au fromage

CHEESE SOUFFLÉ

This is the classic French soufflé, the simplest and the easiest since the cheese blends smoothly with the egg and does not inhibit the rise. The shape and volume of the cooking dish matters. For this recipe you need a soufflé mould (a straight-sided, round ovenproof china or Pyrex dish), diameter 8–9in. Size is important, as are the straight sides that allow the soufflé to rise evenly above the edge.

Serves 4

½ stick butter
½ cup all-purpose flour
1 cup milk
1 cup grated mature cheese, such as Cantal or Gruyère
¼ teaspoon freshly grated nutmeg
salt and freshly milled pepper
1 tablespoon grated Parmesan cheese
5 eggs, separated

1 First make a béchamel sauce, the basis for all savory soufflés. Over a low heat, melt the butter in a small heavy-based pan, sprinkle in the flour, and cook gently for 2–3 minutes until the mixture looks sandy. Whisk in the milk using a wire whisk or beat with a spoon until the sauce is smooth and thick.

2 Beat in the mature cheese. Season with the nutmeg, salt, and pepper and leave to cool.

3 Meanwhile, prepare a double-thick collar of wax paper about the width of your hand, and tie it firmly around the outside of the 8–9in diameter souffle mould with string. Butter the inside of both the dish and the collar, and dust with the Parmesan.

4 Preheat the oven to 400°F. As soon as the béchamel has cooled, beat in the egg yolks. Whisk the egg whites until stiff but do not over-whisk them or they will become dry and grainy. Fold the whites lightly into the béchamel mixture with a metal spoon. Do not be scared to mix thoroughly, just use light strokes and lift the spoon to make sure you incorporate air.

5 Tip the mixture into the soufflé mould and run a knife around the edge just inside the rim to encourage rising. Bake for 30 minutes without opening the oven door. Remove from the oven as soon as the soufflé is beautifully puffed. Snip the string to release the paper collar and serve without delay.

**VARIATIONS** ~ Other flavorings that can replace or augment the cheese are finely chopped spinach or ham, flaked crab, chopped shrimp, and mushrooms sautéed in butter.

# *croque monsieur*

## TOASTED CHEESE AND HAM SANDWICH

France's favorite toastie was first served, says Larousse Gastronomique, *in 1910 in a café in Paris, the Boulevard de Capucines, and remains a popular café snack throughout the land. As a hot hors d'œuvre, it has the advantage of being quickly prepared with ingredients easily to hand. The desirable crunchiness that gives the preparation its name is best achieved by frying in butter with a little olive oil. You may, if you wish, butter the bread on both sides and toast it instead. The ham can be replaced by cooked chicken. When topped with a poached egg, monsieur becomes madame—for reasons I'm sure you can work out for yourself.*

Serves 4

**8 slices day-old bread off a sandwich loaf or tin loaf**
**about 1 stick sweet butter, softened**
**4 slices mature cheese, such as Cantal or Gruyère**
**4 slices smoked ham**
**2–3 tablespoons olive oil**

1 Spread the bread lightly with softened butter—you'll need about half—and sandwich them together with the cheese and ham. Remove the crusts.

2 Melt the remaining butter with the olive oil in a skillet. Fry the sandwiches over a medium heat, turning them once, until the cheese has melted and the bread is deliciously crisp and golden brown.

**NOTE** ~ For a more substantial dish—a light lunch or simple supper—cover the finished croques with a cheese-flavored béchamel, sprinkle with grated cheese, and slip under a preheated broiler to bubble and brown.

# salade de fromage de chèvre chaud

## WARM GOAT'S CHEESE SALAD

This simple little salad is the standby of every rural restaurant in the southern regions of France—goat-country—where the little curd-cheeses known as tommes (a name also applied to similar preparations of sheep's and cow's milk) are traditionally prepared and sold by the goat-keepers themselves. Creamy little cakes, about the size of a baby's fist, of freshly pressed curd, you will see them displayed on trays in every marketplace. They are sold plain, or dusted with thyme, rosemary, or crushed multi-colored peppercorns. They are also sold at various stages of maturity—bloomed, wrinkled, or hardened. The fresh tommes needed for this recipe have not had a chance to mature and they taste of the particular herbs and leaves that have pastured the goats. The flavor is so place specific that a local palate would expect to be able to distinguish between a fresh tomme made from the milk of a flock pastured on one or other side of the mountain.

Serves 4

**2 well-drained tommes or small fresh goat's cheese**
**4 slices day-old baguette**
**about 6 tablespoons olive oil**
**1 frisée lettuce or any bitter salad leaves**
**1 large cube stale bread, rubbed with garlic**
**about 2 tablespoons wine vinegar**
**1 teaspoon sea salt (sel de Guerande, for the flavor)**

1 Preheat the broiler on the hottest setting or the oven to
425°F. Split the cheeses in half horizontally. Toast the baguette
slices lightly on both sides, trickle with oil and top each with a
round of cheese.

2 Place the salad leaves in a salad bowl with the garlic-rubbed
bread. (This piece of bread is the chapon: an integral part of
the French salad bowl, it is designed to perfume the leaves but is
never eaten.)

3 Mix the vinegar with the salt and work it with a fork until the
granules dissolve. Then fork in the olive oil. Toss the salad
with this dressing.

4 Place the cheese-topped bread rounds in the hot oven for
3–4 minutes to melt and bubble, or toast them under the
broiler. Slip them on to the salad and serve without delay (taking
care not to eat the chapon).

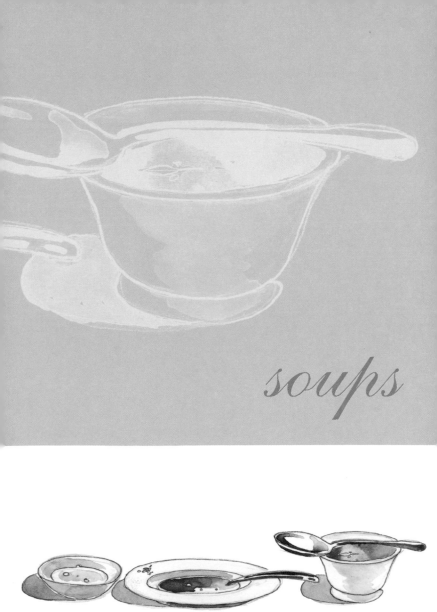

*soups*

# consommé

## CLEAR BEEF BROTH

A basic beef broth which has been concentrated, fortified, and clarified, this is one of those simple preparations by which you can judge the excellence of a chef's kitchen. A consommé can be served plain, or used as the basis for other soups, veloutés, and broths.

Makes about 5¼ pints

**4lb beef bones, chopped into chunks**
**1 chicken carcass (bones only) or 1lb 2oz chicken wings**
**1lb carrots, scraped and cut into chunks**
**1lb leeks, rinsed and cut into chunks**
**2 onions, unpeeled but quartered**
**2–3 celery sticks, cut into chunks**
**a small bunch of bay, parsley, and thyme**
**½ teaspoon white peppercorns**
**salt**

TO FORTIFY
**2lb lean shin of beef, cut into chunks**
**1 tablespoon chopped tomato (optional)**

TO CLARIFY
**3 egg whites, well whisked**

∽

1 Preheat the oven to 350°F. Place the beef bones in a roasting pan and bake for 30 minutes, until well browned.

2 Transfer the bones to a large soup pot. Add the chicken carcass, carrots, leeks, onions, celery, herbs, and peppercorns. Pour in 12 cups water. Bring gently to the boil, allow one big belch, and turn down the heat so that the liquid simmers. Cover loosely and leave to cook gently for 2 hours or so, until well flavored and strong. The surface of the liquid should tremble, no more.

3 Strain the broth, discard the solids, and leave the broth to cool, overnight if possible. Skim off the fat that rises and solidifies overnight.

4 To fortify the broth, return it to the pot and add the shin of beef. Bring to the boil and leave to cook gently for another 2 hours, until the meat has given up all its goodness and the broth has reduced by half. If the color is not sufficiently golden, add the chopped tomato.

5 Strain, discarding the bones and return the broth to the pot. (Save the meat for a Hachis Parmentier, see page 214.) Whisk in the egg whites, bring back to the boil and simmer for 20 minutes. The egg white will float to the surface, collecting all the impurities on the way and leaving a broth of sparkling clarity.

6 Remove from the heat and strain through a fine cheesecloth cloth. Blot the surface of the broth with paper towels laid over the surface to pick up any golden bubbles of fat that have survived the clarifying. Serve the consommé elegantly, in double-handled soup cups.

**CONSOMMÉ OF GOOD COLOR** ~ The preliminary caramelization of the sugars naturally present in the bone meat during the short roasting, along with the color of the onion skins and carrots, give the broth an appetizing golden tint.

**JELLIED CONSOMMÉ** ~ Leave the soup to cool, chill overnight and serve as a jellied consommé—very Marcel Proust.

## ALL ABOUT CONSOMMÉ

The importance of understanding how to prepare a good consommé cannot be exaggerated—or so chefs of the old school will tell you. Forget the stock cubes, leave the little cartons of ready-made where they belong—on the supermarket shelf. I had my first lesson in the etiquette of the stock-pot in the 1980s, at a time when French was still the language of the kitchen and a training in haute cuisine was the sum of a young chef's ambition—before Fusion took over where Italianate left off. At the time, new to the world of recipe-writing and curious to understand the difference between the domestic and the professional kitchen, I spent a working day in the subterranean kitchen of Michel Bourdin, chef de cuisine at the Connaught Hotel in London. In those days, they didn't come much more professional than Chef Bourdin. The day started at dawn—around 6.30 am in early September —with the preparation of the bones for the stock which would serve as the basis for the consommé to be served that evening in the restaurant. Enormous trays of gigantic red-hot bones were whirled around the kitchen with scrupulous politeness by brawny-armed chefs whose qualifications seemed better suited to weight-lifting than dainty behaviour with a whisk. The spitting, steaming mass, smelling deliciously of caramelized meat, was tipped into vats the size of a sherry-barrel and left to bubble and brood all day. These preliminaries were, however, as nothing compared to the Herculean labor of straining and clarifying, a task which involved the entire brawny-armed brigade. "And that," said Michel Bourdin, sipping his tasting-spoon with satisfaction, "is the difference between the housewife and the chef."

# velouté de volaille

## CREAM OF CHICKEN SOUP

This velvet-smooth chicken soup thickened with egg yolk and enriched with cream is one of the glories of the French kitchen. A strong, home-made chicken stock is the secret.

Serves 4

**4 cups chicken stock**
**1 boneless chicken breast, skinned**
**3 egg yolks**
**about 6 tablespoons crème fraîche**
**2 tablespoons sweet butter**
**¼ cup all-purpose flour**
**¼ teaspoon freshly grated nutmeg**
**salt and freshly milled pepper**

1 Heat the chicken stock until it is boiling. Add the chicken breast and poach it for 8–12 minutes, depending on size, until firm and cooked right through.

2 Remove the chicken breast and shred it roughly. Reserve a tablespoonful of the shreds, puree the remainder in a blender with a ladleful of the stock, the egg yolks, and the cream until smooth and liquid. Reserve this puree.

3 Melt the butter in a roomy pan, stir in the flour, and fry until the mixture is sandy, but do not let it brown. Gradually whisk in the broth and simmer gently until it thickens.

4 Remove the pan from the heat and whisk in the pureed chicken and cream mixture. Reheat gently, whisking all the while, until the soup is just below boiling point. Taste and season with nutmeg, salt, and pepper. Return the reserved shredded chicken to the soup and serve without reheating.

**VARIATION** ~ To make a velouté with asparagus or artichoke hearts, prepare the vegetables as usual, removing all woody bits, and poach them in the stock instead of the chicken breast. Finish as in the main recipe, pureeing the vegetables with the cream and egg yolks.

# potage germiny

## CHILLED SORREL SOUP

**G**ather your own sorrel from the wild if you can't find it anywhere else—the pointed, heart-shaped dark green leaves are unmistakeable. Although the substitution of watercress and a squeeze of lemon juice will fool all but the keenest palate, once you've acquired a taste for its refreshing sharpness, nothing else will do.

Serves 4–6

**2 generous handfuls sorrel leaves, rinsed and shredded**
**2 tablespoons butter**
**4 cups strong chicken stock**
**¼ cup all-purpose flour**
**½ cup crème fraîche**
**salt and freshly milled pepper**

TO FINISH
**a little crème fraîche**
**a few sorrel leaves, shredded**
**croûtons, fried in olive oil and butter**

1 Place the sorrel in a pan with a pinch of salt and the butter. Cover tightly and shake over the heat for 2–3 minutes, until the leaves collapse.

2 Puree the contents of the pan in a blender with the chicken stock and flour until smooth. (Alternatively, finely chop the sorrel, mix it with the flour, and add the stock.) Pour the mixture back into the pan and bring to the boil, whisking until the soup thickens a little and no longer tastes of raw flour.

3 Whisk in the crème fraîche. Check the seasoning and add salt and pepper. Remove the pan from the heat and leave to cool. Then chill the soup.

4 Serve the chilled soup topped with a swirl of crème fraîche and a curl of shredded fresh sorrel. For a contrast of texture, hand a bowl of hot croutons separately.

# soupe à l'oignon

## ONION SOUP

A clear bone stock, thick with onions, was the early-morning refreshment in Les Halles, Paris's meat-market. The market has now moved to the outskirts, but when it was at Les Halles in the city centre (and still there in the late 1950s) students from the Sorbonne (myself on occasion among them) would join the porters and wholesalers at the communal wooden tables in the surrounding cafés. A marmite—a deep, round-bellied earthenware cooking pot—is the traditional implement for a heavy, slow simmered soup such as this.

Serves 4–6

**1½lb onions, very finely sliced in rings**
**6 tablespoons butter**
**½ cup white wine**
**3 cups strong beef-bone stock**
**salt and freshly milled pepper**

### TO FINISH
**1½ cups grated cheese, such as Cantal, Gruyère, or Emmenthal**
**4–6 thick slices day-old baguette**

1 Fry the onions in the butter. Cook them very gently, stirring every now and then, for at least 20 minutes, until they are soft and golden.

2 Add the wine. Bring to the boil and bubble up for a few minutes to evaporate the alcohol. Pour in the stock and 1¼ cups cold water, and season with salt and pepper. Bring back to the boil and turn the heat down to simmer the soup. Leave on a low heat for 20 minutes.

3 Meanwhile, preheat the oven to 300°F. Put the baguette slices in the oven to dry. Divide the bread among soup bowls, then ladle in the hot soup: the bread will rise to the top. Either preheat the broiler and top the bread with the cheese, then place the bowls under the broiler to melt and brown the cheese, or hand out a whole piece of cheese and grater for people to add their own, as they liked it in Les Halles.

**NOTE** ~ For a more substantial soup, thicken the cooked broth with 2 eggs beaten with a ladleful of the hot soup, and reheat without boiling.

# *vichyssoise*

## CHILLED LEEK AND POTATO SOUP

A recipe of relatively modern date (a century, no more), this is a refinement of the classic leek and potato soup invented by a French chef from the Bourbonnais working in the US. In the original, the enrichment is butter rather than cream, and it is served hot rather than chilled. Vichyssoise is good with radishes and hot, buttery garlic bread.

Serves 4–6

**2 large leeks, white part only, finely sliced**
**2 large potatoes, peeled and cut into chunks**
**a small bunch of bay, parsley, and thyme**
**½ cup créme fraîche**
**salt and freshly milled pepper**

TO FINISH
**snipped chives**

1 Simmer the leeks and potatoes in 4 cups water with the herbs and a little salt for 30–40 minutes, until the vegetables are very tender.

2 Remove the herbs and puree the soup until smooth in a blender. Taste and add salt and pepper. Cool, then whisk in the crème fraîche and chill the soup. Finish with a sprinkling of chives when serving.

**GARLIC BREAD** ~ To prepare garlic bread, cut diagonal slits in a day-old baguette and fill the slashes with sweet butter mashed with a little garlic—the fresher the garlic, the gentler the flavor. Wrap the baguette in foil or not, as you please: unwrapped, the crust will be crispier; the risk is the loss of some of the butter. Pop the baguette in a preheated oven at 350°F and heat for about 20 minutes, until the butter has melted and soaked into the crumb.

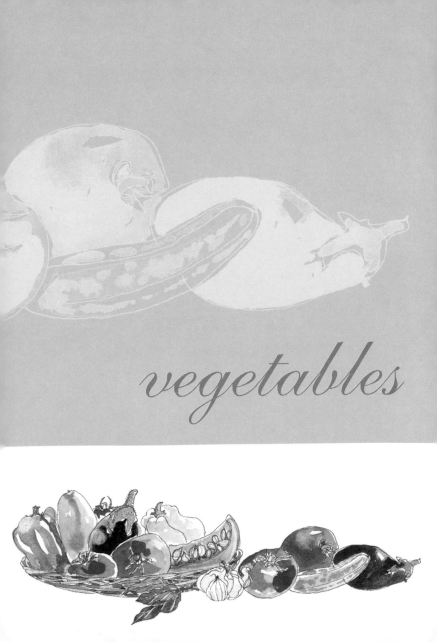

*vegetables*

# pommes de terre sautées

## SAUTÉED POTATOES

Potatoes, butter, and parsley are all you need for this sumptuous little recipe from northern France, dairy country, where butter—rather than the olive oil of the south or the goose fat of central France—is the frying fat of choice. French sweet butter produces very little residue when melted, giving it a relatively high burn point, which makes it perfect for a high-heat sauté—a term which, translated literally, means jump-in-the-pan. Sautéed potatoes are good with grilled lamb cutlets or a steak finished with maître-d'hôtel butter (see page 252).

Serves 4

**2½lb potatoes, scrubbed not peeled**
**1 stick sweet butter**
**salt and freshly milled pepper**
**2 tablespoons chopped flat-leaf parsley**

1 Cook the potatoes until soft in enough boiling salted water to cover them generously. This takes 20 minutes or so. Drain the potatoes, return them to the pan and shake over the heat to dry them out completely. Set the potatoes aside off the heat. Peel them as soon as they are cool enough to handle and slice thickly.

2 Melt the butter in a roomy sauté pan or heavy skillet. Put in the potato slices, season with salt and pepper, and fry briskly for 8–10 minutes, turning the slices carefully to brown both sides. Sprinkle with parsley just before serving.

# *pommes de terre à la boulangère*

## BREAD-OVEN POTATOES

In the old days, before ordinary households acquired their own ovens, dishes such as this one that required baking—a luxurious method—were taken to the village baker's cooling oven after the day's bread-baking was done. The service was offered for a small fee and the title persists though the service is no longer required.

Serves 4–6

**½ stick butter**
**2 onions, finely sliced**
**¾ cup diced fatty bacon**
**2½lb potatoes, peeled and thinly sliced**
**½ teaspoon thyme leaves**
**1 small piece bay leaf, crumbled**
**about 2½ cups boiling stock (chicken, beef or vegetable)**

*⌒∽⌒*

1 Preheat the oven to 350°F. Heat the butter in a skillet and fry the onions and bacon until the onions are lightly browned.

2 Layer the potatoes, bacon, and onion mixture and herbs in a roomy gratin dish. Pour in enough boiling stock to cover the ingredients completely.

3 Cover the dish with foil, shiny side down. Transfer to the oven and bake for 30 minutes. Remove the foil and bake for a further 15–30 minutes, until the potatoes are tender and browned on top.

# gratin dauphinois

## POTATOES BAKED *with* CREAM

This is one of the most delicious and simplest of all potato dishes. The combination of cream and potatoes needs nothing more than a light seasoning with garlic and nutmeg. No cheese, no eggs, though traditionalists usually include a finely sliced turnip. The thickness of the potato slices dictates the time it takes to cook.

Serves 4–6

2½lb waxy potatoes, peeled and sliced
1 garlic clove
1 small turnip, peeled and finely sliced
salt and freshly milled pepper
½ teaspoon freshly grated nutmeg
about 2½ cups light cream
a walnut-sized nugget of butter

1  Preheat the oven to 300°F. Choose a gratin dish just large and deep enough to accommodate the potato slices in 3–4 layers. Cut the garlic in two and rub it around the dish. Lay the potato and turnip slices in the dish, sprinkling between the layers with salt, pepper, and nutmeg.

2  Heat the cream until boiling and pour it over the potatoes, adding just enough to submerge the slices. Dot with a few scraps of butter and cover tightly with a lid or foil, placing the shiny side down.

3  Bake for 1–1½ hours, until the potatoes are perfectly tender and have drunk up almost all the cream. Test for tenderness with a knife after 1 hour. For the final 15 minutes, uncover and turn up the heat to 400–425°F so the top browns and bubbles.

# pommes de terre mousseline

## CREAMY MASHED POTATOES

France's mashed potatoes are enriched with egg yolk and cream, and flavored with nutmeg—they are far richer and more delicious than English mash. Choose medium potatoes of the same size so they cook evenly. If the potatoes are very large, do not boil them but bake them in their jackets and scoop out the soft interior.

Serves 4–6

2½lb potatoes, scrubbed not peeled
1½ sticks sweet butter, softened
4 egg yolks
scant 1 cup whipping cream, whipped
salt and freshly milled white pepper
½ teaspoon freshly grated nutmeg

TO FINISH (OPTIONAL)
chopped fresh herbs, such as parsley, chervil, and/or chives
a little melted butter

1 Cook the potatoes in plenty of boiling salted water until perfectly tender—25–30 minutes. Drain thoroughly and shake them over the heat for a moment to evaporate excess moisture.

2 As soon as they are cool enough to handle, peel the potatoes and push them through a mouli-legumes, potato ricer, or mash and sieve them. Return the mash to the pan, reheat gently and beat in the butter. Remove from the heat and beat in the egg yolks. Fold in the cream. Taste and season with salt, pepper, and nutmeg.

3 To serve plain, pile in a warm dish and finish with a shower of chopped green herbs. To serve with a crisp topping, first preheat the oven to 400°F. Spread the potatoes in a gratin dish, sprinkle with melted butter and bake for 10 minutes, until lightly browned and bubbling.

**DUCHESSE POTATOES** ~ Omit the finishing cream and use a star-shaped piping tube to pipe little pyramids of the hot mousseline on to a buttered baking sheet, sprinkle with a little melted butter and bake as above.

**POTATO CROQUETTES** ~ Allow the mousseline to cool and firm before forming it into little cork-shaped patties. Roll the patties lightly in flour, dip them in egg and bread crumbs, and set aside for 10 minutes to allow the coating to firm. Then deep fry until brown and crisp.

# pommes de terre salardaises

## POTATOES BROWNED IN GOOSE DRIPPING

*P*otatoes browned in confit fat, this is a winter recipe from
the Périgord, the land of the fattened goose. When served
with a grilled magret de canard or d'oie (duck or goose breast),
it is the defining dish of the region. You can buy goose fat in a
tin (a cheaper option than buying the whole confit) or save the
drippings when roasting your Christmas goose or Sunday duck.
If you roast the bird on a rack set over a roasting pan with a
little water, the fat will stay white and won't burn. As a special
treat during the black truffle season (late November to early
March) you might like to include a few slivers of fresh truffle.

Serves 4

**3 tablespoons goose or duck dripping**
**2½lb potatoes, peeled and cut into bite-sized chunks**
**4 garlic cloves, cut into slivers, or 1 large onion, sliced**
**into fine half-moons**
**salt and freshly milled pepper**
**2 tablespoons chopped flat-leaf parsley**

1 Heat the dripping in a roomy sauté pan. As soon as the fat begins to sizzle and yield up its water, add the potatoes and toss over a gentle heat for 10 minutes, until they begin to brown.

2 Add the garlic or onion and a wine glass of water. Season with salt and pepper, bubble up, and cook gently for another 10–15 minutes. Break up the potatoes with a fork, crumbling them a little as soon as they soften, but do not mash.

3 Continue to cook gently, stirring, until the water has evaporated and everything starts to fry again. Stir in the parsley and remove from the heat. The potatoes should have absorbed all the goose fat, retained a little shape, and be deliciously golden and soft.

# aligot

## POTATOES *with* CHEESE

A remarkable dish from the ravines of the Auvergne, this is traditionally served at weddings. Peasant cooking at its most robust: when this dish appears on elegant restaurant menus (as it sometimes does), you can be sure the chef is from the region and had the recipe from his granny. The correct cheese is the local tomme de Cantal, though Emmenthal or Gruyère will do. The more you beat it, the lighter it will be.

❧

### Serves 4–6

**2½lb floury potatoes**
**1 garlic clove, halved**
**⅔ cup heavy cream**
**1 stick sweet butter, diced**
**1lb tomme de Cantal, cut into slivers**
**salt**

1 Boil the potatoes in their jackets in enough salted water to cover. Start with cold water and, about 20 minutes after the water reaches the boil, when perfectly tender, drain the potatoes. Leave until just cool enough to handle.

2 Slip off their skins and return the potatoes to the pan. Set the pan over a low heat and mash the potatoes thoroughly.

3 Meanwhile, rub a heavy pan with the cut side of the garlic clove (discard the rest—a little garlic goes a long way and you don't want to drown the flavor of the cheese). In the garlicky pan, bring the cream and the butter gently to the boil. As soon as the butter melts, beat in the mashed potato.

4 When the potatoes are steaming, add the cheese and beat it in with a wooden spoon or spatula, lifting the utensil high to incorporate as much air as possible. Serve as soon as the cheese has completely melted and the mixture is light and fluffy, as it rapidly loses its volume.

**SERVING TIP** ~ Aligot is delicious but rich. If you value your digestion, don't serve it with wine or anything chilled. Instead, advise your guests to take nothing until they have eaten their fill. Then pour them a nip of white brandy—eau de vie de prune, framboise or poire—to settle the stomach.

# petits pois à la française

BABY PEAS *with* ONIONS AND LETTUCE

*A dish of slow-simmered peas, this is always served as a separate course, handed around after the meat. The long, gentle cooking works its magic on frozen peas as well as fresh.*

∽

Serves 4

1½lb shelled young peas
8 very small baby onions, skinned
1 small romaine lettuce, shredded
a few parsley and chervil sprigs, tied in a bunch
½ cup white wine or water (or a mixture)
a walnut-sized nugget of sweet butter
1 tablespoon sugar
1 teaspoon salt

TO FINISH
a walnut-sized nugget of sweet butter, chopped in small pieces

1 Put all the ingredients (except the butter for finishing) in a heavy-based pan. Bring to the boil and bubble up for a moment to evaporate the alcohol if using wine.

2 Cover and simmer gently for 30–40 minutes, until the peas have lost their fresh green color and the cooking juices are reduced to a couple of tablespoonfuls. Remove the bunch of herbs and stir in the finishing butter.

**VARIATIONS** ~ For petits pois à la bonne femme, proceed as above, but omit the lettuce. Replace the wine with chicken stock and include a tablespoon of diced raw ham or lean bacon.

For petits pois à la fermière, proceed as above, but include a handful of baby carrots.

# confit d'oignons

## CARAMELIZED ONIONS

M*ild, sweet red onions are becoming widely available—
although you can make this with ordinary onions if you
cannot find reds. Make this a day ahead if you like but no sooner.*

∽∾

Makes about 2½ cups

**½ stick sweet butter
6 tablespoons brown sugar
6 large red onions, finely sliced
2 tablespoons red wine vinegar
2 tablespoons red wine
1 tablespoon honey**

∽∾

1 Melt the butter in a heavy pan and stir in the sugar. Stir over
a medium heat for 10 minutes (as if making fudge—if that
helps to explain). When the mixture caramelizes to a light brown,
stir in the sliced onions, vinegar, and wine. Add a splash of water
and bring to the boil.

2 Turn down the heat, cover, and leave to simmer for another
15 minutes, until the onions are soft. Remove from the heat,
season, and stir in the honey.

# *purée d'ail à la crème*

## GARLIC PUREE *with* CREAM

Fragrant, smooth, rich, and delicate, this puree is the perfect accompaniment for plain-grilled meats or spooned over a fried egg. Best made with fresh garlic, whose cloves have just formed, when the covering will still be soft and the cloves plump and mild-flavored. If using elderly garlic, halve the cloves first and nick out the little green sprout at the heart.

Serves 4–6

**10 heads fresh garlic**
**½ cup heavy cream**
**salt and freshly milled pepper**

1 Peel the garlic cloves and put them in enough boiling salted water to cover. Let them simmer for 10 minutes. Drain. If the garlic is a little elderly, allow another 5 minutes.

2 Puree the garlic by pushing it through a mouli-legume, potato ricer, and then beat in the cream. Alternatively, puree both garlic and cream in a blender until smooth. Reheat to serve and season with salt and pepper.

# tomates à la provençale

## TOMATOES SLOW-COOKED *with* GARLIC

A simple recipe, but perfect of its kind. The tomatoes can only achieve their concentrated sweetness through long slow cooking—allow them all the time they need. This is delicious served with braised fennel (see opposite).

Serves 4

**8 large ripe beef tomatoes**
**3 tablespoons olive oil**
**2 garlic cloves, peeled**
**salt**
**a handful of flat-leaf parsley**

⌇

1 Cut the tomatoes in half and remove the seeds. Warm the oil in a wide shallow pan. Put the tomatoes in the pan, cut sides down. Fry the tomatoes over the gentlest of heat for 40–45 minutes, shaking the pan from time to time so that they do not stick and burn.

2 Crush the garlic with salt, and then mince it very finely with the parsley. Turn the tomatoes over, and sprinkle them with salt, garlic, and parsley. Let them continue to cook very, very gently on the other side—another 30 minutes is not too long.

**BRAISED FENNEL** ~ Trim and quarter the bulbs and lay them in a single layer in a gratin dish. Sprinkle with lemon juice and add enough stock or white wine and water to come half way up the bulbs. Dot with butter, season, cover with foil (shiny side down) and bake in the oven at 350°F for 1 hour, until the fennel is perfectly soft.

# carottes vichy

## CARROTS *with* BUTTER AND PARSLEY

The defining ingredients here are sugar and either baking soda—known in France as Vichy salt—or Vichy water, a bottled water with a strong mineral flavor, much esteemed for health reasons. The French housewife doesn't like her vegetables undercooked and chewy: she likes them well-cooked and soft. She might, at the beginning of the season when the primeurs, the early baby vegetables, arrive in the market, choose not to cook the tender young things at all but present them as crudités—raw vegetables—and serve them as an hors d'œuvre with a mayonnaise. When cooked, green vegetables are usually steamed rather than boiled, drained as soon as they're soft, passed under the cold tap to halt the cooking process, then reheated as needed in generous amounts of butter.

Serves 4–6

**2lb young carrots, scraped and finely sliced**
**¹/₂ cup mineral water, preferably Vichy Saint-Yorre**
**1 teaspoon sugar**
**½ stick sweet butter**
**salt and freshly milled pepper**
**1 tablespoon chopped parsley**

1 Put the sliced carrots into a heavy pan with the mineral water, sugar, and a small piece of the butter—about the size of a hazelnut. Season with salt and pepper, bring to the boil and cover tightly.

2 Turn the heat right down and cook gently until all the liquid has been absorbed and the carrots are perfectly tender—10–15 minutes. Remove the lid at the end of cooking and shake the pan over the heat to evaporate any remaining liquid.

3 Chop the remaining butter into small pieces. When you are ready to serve the carrots, toss them with the butter and parsley—both should retain their freshness.

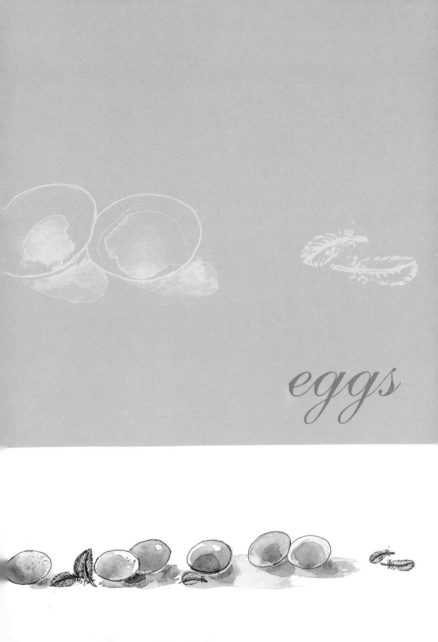

*eggs*

# œufs à la coque

## SOFT-COOKED EGGS

If you do not have eggs from your own hens, choose free-range eggs from a reliable source. A perfectly soft-cooked egg is a fine-judged thing—down to a matter of seconds of cooking time. If the eggs have been refrigerated, allow them to come to room temperature before you start. In France, egg cups are not generally provided—you'll be expected to peel the eggs and eat them with a fork rather than slice off the top and eat the contents of the shell with a spoon.

Serves 1

**2 eggs**

1 Bring a large pan of water to the boil. When it is boiling, remove it from the heat and slip in the eggs. Return the pan to the heat, cover, and allow to simmer.

2 For a softly-set white and a runny yolk, remove the eggs with a draining spoon after 3–3½ minutes, depending on the size of the eggs. If you leave the eggs in the water for 1½ minutes longer, you will have œufs mollets: plunge them immediately into cold water and then peel them, when you'll find the whites will be firm and the yolks still soft.

**NOTE** ~ The eggs are delicious salted and peppered as a dipping sauce for asparagus spears.

# œufs en gelée

POACHED EGGS *in* ASPIC

This simple recipe depends on a well-flavored aspic based on a strong consommé (see page 74), set either by the inclusion of a couple of veal knuckles or calf's foot in the basic stock, or with good-quality gelatine from a packet. Gelatine is available as crystals or as leaves—follow the instructions on the packet, making sure you soak the gelatine in cold water until it swells before you add it to the hot consommé, then mix well to blend thoroughly.

❧

Serves 4

8 very fresh free-range eggs
2 tablespoons wine vinegar
2–3 fine slices ham, cut into thin strips
2½ cups aspic jelly, cooled to a soft set
8 small fresh tarragon sprigs or large leaves

1 Have ready eight little ramekins and a bowl of iced water. Crack one of the eggs into a cup. Bring 4 cups water to the boil in a roomy pan, such as a sauté pan or fairly deep skillet. Add the vinegar (no salt as this will make the egg white separate) and bubble up again.

2 Turn the heat down so that the water simmers. Use a spoon to swirl the water into a whirlpool and slip in the egg from the cup, into the middle of the whirlpool. Prepare another in the same way and slip it in. Allow the eggs to poach for 3–4 minutes, keeping the water at a low simmer, then remove with a draining spoon and transfer to the iced water. Continue until all the eggs are cooked. Trim the eggs of any stray wisps of white.

3 Dip a few strips of ham in the aspic jelly and divide among the ramekins. Place a well-drained poached egg in each ramekin, surround with the remaining ham, and top with a small sprig (or single large leaf) of tarragon. Cover the eggs with the aspic and transfer the ramekins to the fridge to set.

4 Unmould the eggs to serve or leave them in the ramekins. To unmould an egg, rinse a tea towel in very hot water and wrap it around the outside of the ramekin for a few seconds, remove the cloth, and cover with a plate. Invert both ramekin and plate, then lift off the ramekin.

# œufs pochés meurette

## EGGS POACHED *in* RED WINE

*I*n this traditional recipe from the vineyards of Burgundy, eggs poached in red wine take on a dramatically dark red skin, veiling the white. The poaching liquid is then reduced to a rich, shiny glaze without any additional thickening.

❧

Serves 4

1 bottle red Burgundy or any heavy red wine
8 fresh free-range eggs
8 small rounds day-old bread (the right size for a poached egg)
1 stick sweet butter, chilled
2 tablespoons diced lean bacon
2 tablespoons finely chopped shallot or onion

1 Bring the wine to the boil in a roomy pan, such as a sauté
pan or fairly deep skillet. Reduce the heat so that the wine
simmers. Break the eggs one by one into a cup and slip them into
the simmering wine—cooking no more than two at a time is
safest. Keep the wine simmering gently and allow 3–4 minutes
cooking time. Remove each egg with a draining spoon as soon as
the white has set and transfer it to a round of bread. Trim the
egg to a neat shape and reserve.

2 In another pan, melt half the butter and fry the bacon and
chopped shallot or onion for a few minutes—just long enough
to soften (do not let them take color).

3 Strain the poaching wine over the bacon mixture, bring to the
boil, and bubble fiercely for 15–20 minutes, until the liquid is
reduced by half.

4 Chop the chilled butter into small pieces. Remove the pan
from the heat and gradually whisk in the bits of chilled butter
to thicken the sauce and give it a shine.

5 Pour the sauce over the eggs. Do not worry if the eggs look a
little gray—the sauce solves the problem. Serve immediately.

# œufs brouillés aux truffes

## SCRAMBLED EGGS *with* TRUFFLES

Egg shells, being porous, soak up the scent of a truffle like a sponge. So the canny truffle-hunter who intends to take his truffles to market next day buries them among a few fresh eggs overnight—one way to have your cake and eat it. Even better, though undeniably less profitable, is to scramble the eggs with the truffle.

∽

Serves 4 as an hors d'œuvre

**8 perfectly fresh free-range eggs**
**1 fine black truffle, about 2oz**
**½ stick sweet butter**
**salt and freshly milled pepper**

TO FINISH
**2 tablespoons sweet butter, chilled and finely diced**
**fresh baguette or croutons fried in butter until crisp**

1 Bury the truffle in the eggs overnight in a tightly covered jar. Next day, brush any soil off the truffle (do not rinse it unless this is really necessary) and cut it into fine matchstick slivers.

2 Crack the eggs into a bowl and fork them briefly to blend the yolk and white—do not beat them. Season the eggs with salt and pepper.

3 Melt the butter gently in a heavy pan without letting it brown. When it froths, add the truffle and toss it over the heat for 1 minute, no more.

4 Stir in the eggs and cook the mixture very gently, moving the base with a wooden spoon, until the eggs form creamy curds. Dot with the cold butter to halt the cooking process and serve immediately, with chunks of fresh baguette or croutons.

# œufs en cocotte à la crème

## BAKED EGGS *with* CREAM

For absolute authenticity, you need those little cocotte dishes with a single handle (ovenproof china, white on the inside, brown on the outside—very 1960s), though one-person soufflé dishes will do.

Serves 4 as a starter

**8 very fresh free-range eggs**
**¾ cup heavy cream**
**salt and freshly milled white pepper**

1 Preheat the oven to 400°F. Crack the eggs into eight ramekins or cocotte dishes (one egg per dish) or four individual soufflé dishes (two per dish). Drop a spoonful of cream in each dish and season lightly with salt and freshly milled white pepper. Do not butter the containers first or the egg will fry and harden instead of being tender and creamy.

2 Arrange the dishes in a bain-marie, a roasting pan with enough boiling water to come half way up the dishes. Bake for 6–8 minutes, until the eggs are softly set and still creamy. Serve without delay as the eggs continue to cook after they come out of the oven.

**TESTING EGGS FOR FRESHNESS** ~ To test an egg for freshness, place it in a bowl of water (unsalted). If the egg remains horizontal and does not bob to the surface, it is perfectly fresh; if it tips towards the vertical and bobs upwards, it is not in the first flush of youth but is still edible; if it floats, it is really not worth eating. Floating has something to do with the presence or lack of air inside the shell: the shell, being porous, gradually allows the liquid-matter inside to evaporate, replacing it with air. A bad egg is unmistakable—the sulphurous smell is overwhelming.

# tian de blea

## BAKED CHARD OMELETE

The Provençal tian—a pastry-less quiche—takes its name from the shallow, round earthenware dish in which it is cooked. Unlike the omelete, however, cooked vegetables are always involved, the most characteristic being chard, beet-greens —drought-resistant spinach-like leaves, much-valued in the Mediterranean kitchen and particularly popular in the region of Nice where they take the place of all other greens. While the leaves are prepared like spinach, the fleshy white stalks are cooked separately and eaten like asparagus with an oil and vinegar dressing or an aïoli for dipping. In Old Nice, the chard tian is known as la trouchia and is sold, cut in thick wedges, in every cooked-food shop as a mid-morning snack.

❧

Serves 4 as a main dish

**1¼lb chard leaves (no stalks) or spinach, trimmed**
**2 tablespoons olive oil**
**1 garlic clove, crushed with a little salt**
**8 eggs**
**½ cup grated strong cheese, such as Cantal or Parmesan**
**½ teaspoon freshly grated nutmeg**
**salt and freshly milled pepper**

1 Preheat the oven to 300°F. Rinse the chard leaves thoroughly and shake dry. Drop them in a roomy pan with 1 tablespoon of the olive oil and the garlic crushed with a little salt. Cover tightly and shake over the heat for 4–5 minutes, until the leaves are wilted.

2 Transfer the chard to a sieve to drain. As soon as the greens are cool enough to handle, squeeze them thoroughly to extract as much moisture as possible. Chop them finely with a sharp knife.

3 Brush a 10in tian or earthenware baking dish with a little of the remaining oil. Crack the eggs into a bowl and fork to blend the yolks and whites. Stir in the chopped leaves and grated cheese, season with nutmeg, salt, and pepper and tip into the baking dish.

4 Transfer to the oven and bake for 35–40 minutes until just set—the tian will cook more as it cools. The low temperature allows the egg to set gently without bubbling. Serve warm or cool.

**VARIATIONS** ~ A fine tian can be made with a ragout of artichoke hearts. Allow one heart per egg and cook them gently until soft with a little white wine, olive oil, and garlic.

Equally good is a tian made with a ratatouille (see page 46) or diced eggplant cooked in olive oil with plenty of sliced onion. The only rule is that the volume of vegetables should equal that of the eggs.

# omelette aux fines herbes

## HERB OMELETE

You need a small skillet, light enough to be easily tipped and kept solely for the purpose. Raw iron is traditional, non-stick the easier modern alternative. The size of the pan dictates the size of the omelete as the eggs take the shape of the pan. A 7–8in pan is suitable for a 2–egg omelete to serve one person. For a 4–egg omelete to serve two, use a 8¾–9½in diameter pan, and so on. The larger the pan, the larger the omelete. In the rural Languedoc, where my children attended school, on Shrove Tuesday (when all the eggs in the larder must be used up before Lent) their schoolmates made an omelete large enough to feed all the children in the village, cooking it in an enormous pan over an open fire in the woods. An omelete is served baveuse—frothy—never well-done. The traditional flavoring herbs are flat-leaf parsley, chives, chervil, and tarragon. Make each omelete individually and serve it straight from the pan. The aim is a perfect little rolled bolster, soft in the middle and tenderly firm on the outside. For a filled omelete, omit the herbs and replace with a light stuffing, cooked in advance. Drop a spoonful of chopped mushrooms or tomatoes simmered in cream into the heart of the omelete before you flip it over. Or sprinkle with chopped ham or grated cheese.

Serves 1

**2 free-range eggs**
**a walnut-size piece of butter**
**1 tablespoon freshly chopped soft-leafed herbs**
**salt and freshly milled pepper**

1 Set a plate to warm before you begin. The omelete must be served as soon as it comes out of the pan.

2 Fork up the eggs with the herbs, a little salt, and a generous turn of the pepper mill. The eggs should be frothy, but not thoroughly whisked.

3 Melt half the butter in a small omelete pan. The heat should be high, but not too high. When the butter foams but before it turns brown, roll it around the base and tip in the egg. Holding the handle with one hand and the fork with the other, move the eggs as they cook, drawing the set egg from the base of the pan in soft creamy curds, much as for scrambled eggs. After a moment, when the curds are just formed but still frothy, stop moving it so a skin can form on the base.

4 Drop the rest of the butter on the froth. Fold a third of the omelete over the middle third. Tip it out on to the warm plate, allowing the folded third to fold on to the open third to create a plump, oblong bolster. The omelete should be lightly browned on the outside but still juicy inside. The cooking should take no more than 1 minute—my tester says 30 seconds!

# quiche lorraine

## EGG AND BACON TART

This is the original quiche—an open-topped tart filled with a savory custard—which takes its name from Germany's kuchen, the generic name for a cake. The original pastry base was a bread dough; the modern version is either shortcrust, as here, or puff pastry. I think it works best with shortcrust—not least because it is easy, quick, and minimizes the temptation to use ready-made. Home-made is really well worth the effort.

Serves 4

**1½ cups all-purpose flour**
**½ teaspoons salt**
**1 stick sweet butter, chilled**
**1 egg yolk**

FILLING
**1 cup finely diced lean bacon or salted belly pork**
**1 tablespoon butter**
**4 eggs, forked together**
**1 cup heavy cream**
**¼ teaspoon freshly grated nutmeg**
**salt and freshly milled pepper**

1 First make the pastry. Sift the flour into a bowl with the salt and chop or grate in the chilled butter. Rub lightly between your fingertips until the mixture looks like fine bread crumbs.

2 Fork the egg yolk with 2 tablespoons very cold water. Still using the tips of your fingers, work the yolk mixture into the dry ingredients and press the mixture together to make a firm ball of dough, adding a further 1 tablespoon water only if necessary. Do not overwork. (You can make the pastry in a food processor if you prefer.) Wrap the dough in plastic wrap and set it in a cool place for 30 minutes.

3 Preheat the oven to 400°F. Have ready a 10in round tart pan, preferably one with a removable base. Tip the pastry-ball on to a floured board. With a floured rolling pin, roll it out to a

circle about ¼ in thick. Using the rolling pin to support the pastry, transfer it to the tart pan and ease it into the sides—do not stretch the pastry. Trim the pastry, leaving a rim of about 1in to allow for shrinkage. Use trimmings to patch up any holes, pressing them in place with a damp finger.

4 Prick the pastry base with a fork in a few places and line with foil, shiny side down. Drop a few dried beans or rice-grains on the foil to keep it in place. Bake for 10 minutes to set the pastry. Remove the foil and bake for another 5 minutes to dry the surface. Leave to cool.

5 Meanwhile, gently fry the bacon or salted belly pork in the butter until the fat changes color and begins to sizzle (do not let it brown). Leave to cool a little. Fork the eggs with the cream (do not beat), season with nutmeg, salt, and pepper, and stir in the contents of the skillet.

6 Tip the egg mixture into the cooled pastry shell, taking care not to overfill it or let the level come above the edge of the shell. Turn down the oven to 300°F and bake for 25–30 minutes, until the custard is lightly set and the pastry deliciously golden. Serve warm or at room temperature, never chilled.

*Watch a French housewife as she makes her way
slowly along the loaded stalls... searching for
the peak of ripeness and flavor... What you are
seeing is a true artist at work, patiently
assembling all the materials of her craft, just as
the painter squeezes oil colors onto his palette
ready to create a masterpiece.*

**Keith Floyd,** contemporary TV chef and writer

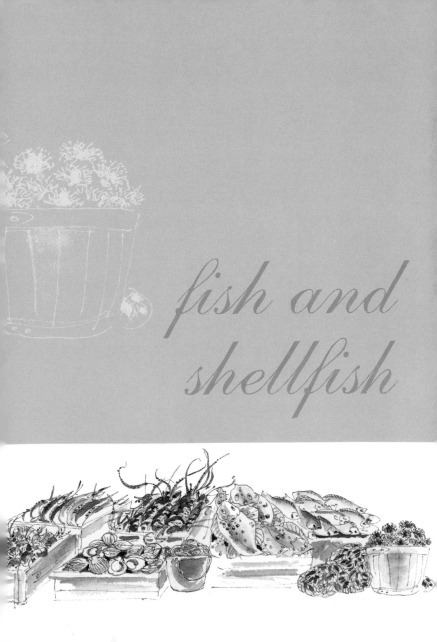

# fish and shellfish

# moules marinières

In its simplest form, the freshly gathered mussels are opened in a closed pan over a heat sufficiently high for the shells to spring open immediately, discharging their liquid and providing the cooking liquor. Shop-bought mussels need a little extra assistance. Bivalves, such as mussels, can stay alive as long as they can hold water in their shells. To discover their condition, drop them in cold water, stir vigorously, watch closely, and discard any that fail to close or remain shut. If in doubt, slide the two halves of the shell across each other: if the mussel is empty, the shells will slip open, revealing sand and debris inside. Mussels are a natural crop which need little or no husbandry. In the wild, they cling to rocks on the tide-line, feeding off whatever floats past. Farmed mussels are farmed only in the sense that the wild spat, free-range at this early stage, are encouraged to establish themselves on a particular support—a post or a rope. To prepare mussels for the pot, rinse thoroughly, scrub vigorously, and—finally, since the mussel won't last long without its beard—use a blunt knife to scrape off the whiskery little black tag which protrudes from the shell. Once bearded, mussels lose water and must be cooked within the hour.

Serves 4

**4lb mussels, scrubbed and bearded**
**½ stick sweet butter**
**1 tablespoon diced jambon cru (raw cured ham)**
**or lean bacon (optional)**
**2 shallots or 1 small onion, finely chopped**
**1 glass white wine**

TO FINISH
**chopped parsley/chopped garlic**
**freshly milled pepper**

1 Rinse the mussels and discard any that do not shut when given a sharp tap.

2 Gently heat half the butter in a roomy pan. Add the jambon cru or bacon and shallots or onion, and leave to fry for a moment to soften (do not let the ingredients brown).

3 Tip in the mussels and the wine, cover tightly and shake over the heat. The shells will pop open in the steam—stir to allow the ones at the top to drop to the bottom and feel the heat. When all the mussels have opened, they are done: remove the pan from the heat immediately (overcooked shellfish quickly toughen).

4 Finish with parsley, garlic, and pepper. Ladle into bowls with their broth. Any grit will have dropped to the bottom of the pot. There is no need to add salt with ham or bacon. Eat with your fingers—one shell can be used to scoop out the other.

**VARIATIONS** ~ For moules à la crème, strain the mussel broth, bubble up to reduce it by a third, and stir in its own volume of double cream, preferably the thick, slightly soured cream of Normandy. Bubble up again before pouring it back over the mussels. For extra richness, stir in a ladleful of béchamel sauce.

For moules à la poulette, strain and bubble up the broth as above, stir in a couple of tablespoons of cream forked with 2 egg yolks. Heat the enriched broth gently in a bowl set over simmering water, whisking until the sauce thickens a little. Season with salt and freshly milled pepper, then pour the sauce back over the mussels (removed from their shells or left on the half-shell, as you please).

For moules frites, remove the mussel meat and marinate in lemon juice for 30 minutes, then dip in your favorite frying batter, and deep fry. Serve with quartered lemons.

Wherever you find mussels, you'll find sea-urchins. Prickly spheres the size of a golf-ball, these little sea-creatures are most commonly encountered when you get a clutch of their needle-like spikes stuck in your foot while exploring the rock pools of the Mediterranean shoreline. By the time you manage to extract the creature's armoury, you'll probably never want to see it again. Which would be a pity because, once you manage to reach the edible parts, the prickly carapace hides one of the great delicacies of the Mediterranean table. Sea urchin corals (actually, the ovaries) are five little scraps of soft, fragrant caviar-flavored flesh not much larger than a fingernail. Arranged in star shape, these are only visible when the creature has been neatly sliced in half, a task which, since it's still alive and very prickly, is best left to those who know what they're doing. A wild-gathered crop, you'll find sea-urchins for sale in Mediterranean seaside markets from September to April. The seller will perform the service of opening the creatures for you. If not, use a protective glove and a pair of garden-clippers, or get yourself a coupe-oursin, specially designed scissors purchaseable in any French ironmongery. Once opened, the tender morsels won't last. You can eat them immediately with a squeeze of lemon, or wait till you get home and eat them folded at the last minute into softly scrambled eggs. Or make an oursinado: stir them into a little sauce of well-reduced white wine thickened with butter and egg yolks; eat with bread, or with poached eggs, or as a sauce for plain, poached fish.

# huîtres au four

## BAKED OYSTERS

The oyster farms of Brittany have been in business since the days of the Romans, when the mollusks were sent overland to the Empire's capital, packed in seaweed and tightly barreled (like all bivalves, they remain alive as long as they can hold water in their shells). Here, their reputation as an aphrodisiac made them in great demand at the feasts of Saturnalia. In France, they remain the festive food of the New Year, when they are sold by the lorry load. Neatly crated, marked and priced by breed and size, the oysters are available from supermarket forecourts throughout the land. For the pleasure of contrast, serve a dozen chilled and a dozen grilled oysters as a appetizer for a celebration supper.

Serves 2

**12 oysters**
**4 tablespoons fresh bread crumbs**
**2 tablespoons white wine or milk**
**4 tablespoons finely chopped shallots**
**1 tablespoon finely chopped parsley**
**salt and freshly milled pepper**
**1 cup grated cheese**

1 Gripping the more cup-like of the shell halves firmly in a cloth, open the oysters by levering the shells apart. This is easiest to do with an oyster opener, a dagger-like instrument with a protective hasp, although a short, strong knife will suffice if you lack the purpose-made tool.

2 Preheat the oven to maximum, or heat the broiler as high as possible. Leaving each on the deepest of its two shells, arrange the oysters in a shallow gratin dish in a single layer.

3 Soak the bread crumbs briefly in the wine or milk to swell, then mix in the chopped shallot and parsley. Season with salt and freshly milled pepper and divide sparingly among the oysters as a topping: the aim is to provide a crisp little hat, not a blanket. Finish with a sprinkling of the grated cheese.

4 Slip the oysters into the top of a hot oven or under a broiler and allow 3–4 minutes cooking—just long enough to melt the cheese and brown the bread crumbs. Serve immediately.

# tellines provençales

## CLAMS IN TOMATO AND OLIVE SAUCE

*I*n Provence, the little purple-tinged clams known as tellines *are the preferred mollusk, although the larger palourdes or any other bivalve can be prepared in this way. Serve without reheating, as shellfish harden if overcooked.*

⤮

Serves 2 as a main dish, 4 as an appetizer

**4lb live shellfish (such as clams, mussels, cockles,
razor shells and queen scallops)**
**½ teaspoon saffron (about 12 strands)**
**4–6 tablespoons olive oil**
**1 large onion, finely chopped**
**3–4 garlic cloves, finely chopped**
**2lb ripe tomatoes, peeled, seeded and diced or canned are fine**
**1 bay leaf**
**1 sprig thyme**
**1 tablespoon pitted black olives, chopped**
**salt and freshly milled pepper**
**a little sugar**
**½ cup white wine**

TO FINISH
**chopped parsley**

1 Rinse the shellfish and leave them in a bucket of cold water for a few hours—overnight is best—to spit out their sand.

2 Toast the saffron in a dry pan for 1–2 minutes until it releases its scent—do not let it burn or it will be bitter. Transfer it to a cup containing a little boiling water. Leave to infuse for 15 minutes or so. This preliminary toasting of the saffron is a refinement supposedly to enhance the flavor—I am not entirely convinced, but try it for yourself.

3 Heat the olive oil in a roomy skillet and fry the onion and garlic until soft and golden—do not let them brown. Add the tomatoes and bubble up, squashing the tomatoes down until they soften.

4 Add the bay leaf, thyme, olives, saffron with its soaking water, and another glass of water. Bubble up again, then turn down the heat and leave to bubble for 20 minutes or so until the sauce is thick and rich.

5 Season with salt, pepper, and a little sugar. Add the wine, bubble up again, and add the raw shellfish. Bubble up once more, cover loosely and let the shells open in the steam, shaking the pan every now and again to allow the top layer to drop to the bottom. Take the pan off the heat as soon as the shells gape open —4–6 minutes, depending on the size of pan and thickness of the shells. Finish with plenty of chopped parsley.

# *coquilles st jacques*
# *sauce mornay*

## SCALLOPS *with* WINE AND CREAM

T he scallop, known as the pilgrim shell for its ability to propel itself through the water by means of a powerful adductor muscle, is a free-range bivalve—most shellfish are sedentary. It grows fine and sweet in the waters of the Atlantic. The curved shell, once emptied and scrubbed, is re-usable as a container for a little gratin of other fish: shrimp, diced fillets of sole, or angler fish.

Serves 4

**8–12 live scallops on the shell**
**1 cup white wine**
**2 tablespoons butter**
**¼ cup all-purpose flour**
**1 cup heavy cream**
**salt and freshly milled pepper**
**¼ teaspoon freshly grated nutmeg**

TO FINISH
**2 tablespoons chopped parsley**
**2 tablespoons fresh bread crumbs**
**1–2 tablespoons melted butter**

1  Rinse and scrub the scallops in their shells. To open, place them round-side down in a shallow pan with enough boiling water to come nearly to the top of the shells, set the pan on the heat and bring the water back to the boil. Alternatively, place the scallops in a roasting pan, add boiling water as in a pan, and transfer to a low oven. After a few moments the shells will open and you'll be able to lever a knife between the two halves, revealing the meat.

2  Remove the frill (the eyes) and the little sandy sack of intestine from the scallop. Slice the white adductor muscle horizontally into 2–3 medallions about ¼ in thick, and put them aside with the coral. Scrub the four largest curved shells and put them aside.

3  Preheat the broiler. Bring the wine to the boil in a small pan. Slide in the white scallop meat and poach for 1½–2 minutes, just long enough for the fish to turn opaque. Remove and reserve. Add the corals to the pan, return the poaching liquid to the boil, cook for 1 minute, remove and reserve.

4  Melt the butter in a small pan until it foams, then sprinkle in the flour. Fry for 1 minute, then add the poaching liquid. Whisk over the heat until the sauce thickens. Then stir in the cream. Taste, season with salt, pepper, and a pinch of nutmeg, and bubble up again.

5  Pour a little of the sauce into each of the four reserved scallop shells, top with the scallop meat and corals, and finish with the remaining sauce. Sprinkle with the chopped parsley and bread crumbs, and trickle with a little melted butter. Slip under the broiler to brown and bubble. Serve very hot.

# *bouillabaisse*

## FISH CHOWDER *with* SAFFRON

The most famous of fish soups is one of those all-in soup-stews served as two or even three courses that form the entire meal. Its invention is attributed to the fish wives of Marseilles and it takes its name, not (as so often with such dishes) from the cooking implement, but from the method. A bouillon-abaissé is a broth whose heat is raised and lowered and then raised again, a process which encourages the broth to form an emulsion with the oil. A dish that speaks to the heart as well *as the stomach, the bouillabaisse satisfies the emotional as well as the practical needs of the participants. As for the correct composition, it is not, in spite of what the chefs of the region will tell you, a recipe set in stone. Nonetheless some things are generally agreed. Extra-virgin olive oil should be used for the enrichment. Saffron is the only essential flavoring. Some fish are suitable, some are not. Shellfish are never included. For strength in the broth, there must be one or more of the rockfish —in France, these are rascasse, rouquier, labre, girelle, demoiselle. In addition to these any collection of small fish sold as "soup fish" will do with the exclusion of sardines, anchovies, and all members of the flat fish family, including sole and turbot, any of which would make the broth bitter. Seven is the minimum number for which it is proper to prepare bouillabaisse, says the great 19th century authority on Provençal cooking, J-B Reboule. As for quantities, he suggests for sharing between two people, 2–3lb fish cooked in 1 liter water, plus 1 tablespoon olive oil per 1lb fish.*

Serves 6–8 as a main course

## THE FISH
**8lb of several different varieties such as:**
**rockfish of the wrasse family (rascasse)**
**sea bass (loup de mer)**
**angler fish (baudroie)**
**scorpion fish (chapon)**
**John Dory or porgy (saint-pierre)**
**conger eel**
**red mullet (rouget)**
**red gurnard (galinette)**
**whiting (merlan)**
**weever fish (vive)**
**spiny lobster (langouste, also known as crawfish, rock lobster)**
**shore crabs: stone, rock, green, blue, oyster or pea crab and red crab**
**shrimp, crayfish**
**skate wings (raie)**
**escalopes or fillets of tuna, turbot, mackerel, bonito**

## THE BASIC BROTH
**bones, heads, trimmings from the above,**
**including whole fish if small**
**3–4 shallots or leeks, chopped**
**3–4 garlic cloves, crushed**
**2 large tomatoes, peeled, seeded, and chopped**
**3–4 sprigs each of fennel, parsley, and thyme**
**a curl of dried orange peel**
**½ teaspoon saffron (about 12 strands)**
**salt and freshly milled pepper**

**3–4 large, oval, yellow-fleshed potatoes, peeled
and quartered horizontally
about 8 tablespoons olive oil**

ROUILLE
**2 red bell peppers, whole or canned, prepared
4 garlic cloves
½ teaspoon salt
1 thick slice dry bread, about 2oz
2 red chili peppers, seeded and chopped**

TO FINISH
**4 dried bread rolls, sliced in half
(in Marseilles, navette a soupe)
1 garlic clove, halved**

✧

1 Scale, trim, and bone the fish as appropriate, reserving the heads and skeletons. Cut the larger fish into pieces roughly the same size as the smaller fish.

2 Divide the fish between two plates. Plate one should have firm fleshed fish, such as rascasse, weaver, gurnard, eel, angler fish, swordfish, and anything else that feels firm to the finger, including any crustaceans. Plate two should have the soft-fleshed fish, such as sea bass, St. Peter's fish, whiting and whatever else that looks like a member of this group.

3 Put the fish debris, shallots or leeks, garlic, tomatoes, herb sprigs, orange peel, and saffron in the cooking pot with 17½ cups water. Bring to the boil, season with salt and freshly

milled pepper, turn down the heat and simmer for 20–30 minutes to extract all the flavor and body from the ingredients. Strain the broth and return it to the pot with the potatoes. Bring all back to the boil.

6 Meanwhile, make the rouille. Preheat the oven to 450°F. Burn off the skin of the peppers by roasting them in the oven for about 15 minutes. Alternatively, burn them over a direct flame until the skin is charred. Place in a plastic bag to soften for 20 minutes, then carefully separate the flesh from the skin with a knife.

5 Crush the garlic with the salt. Soak the bread in a little water and squeeze it dry. Pound the pepper flesh, garlic, bread, and chili peppers to a smooth paste in a mortar with a pestle or in a food processor. Reserve.

6 Set a soup tureen and a large serving dish to warm along with sufficient soup plates. Tell all participants you will be ready to serve in exactly 10 minutes: as with the soufflé, the bouillabaisse waits for no man.

7 As soon as the broth and potatoes have come back to the boil, allow 10 minutes for the potatoes to soften a little. Add the firm-fleshed fish from plate one, starting with the crustaceans. Sprinkle with the olive oil, cover the pot again and bring all swiftly back to the boil. Boil rapidly for 5 minutes.

8 Lay the soft fish from plate two in the pot. Bring all swiftly back to the boil and continue boiling briskly, uncovered, for another 5 minutes.

9 Take the pot off the heat and, using a draining spoon, gently transfer the fish to the serving plate. Stir a ladleful of the hot fish broth into the rouille. Rub the bread rolls with a cut clove of garlic and spread with a little rouille (or hand this separately, as you please), and place the slices in the tureen. Ladle in a little of the broth and wait until the bread goes spongy—a minute or two.

10 Ladle in the rest of the broth. Set the tureen and the fish on the table at the same time. Provide a warm soup plate and a fork and spoon for each guest, along with a large napkin, finger bowls and a communal plate for the little bones. Pass the rest of the rouille separately, with more bread, fresh this time, to accompany. Everyone eats as he or she pleases—soup with fish, soup then fish, anything goes. To accompany the bouillabaise, serve the good red wine of the Rhone valley and encourage your guests to drink up the last of the broth straight from the plate after the addition of a glass of wine—a gesture of appreciation known as faire chabrot.

**NOTES** ~ You may, if you wish, pass around a bowl of aïoli as well as the rouille. Although purists would reject the notion, it is worth it for the dramatic contrast between the fiery scarlet and the soft gold.

If all you have is a handful of bony little fish, make a bouillabaisse borgne—a strong fish broth, served with all its accompaniments, but with a handful of greens and a poached egg substituted for the larger chunks of fish in each portion.

The Corsican equivalent, la zuminu, includes squid, cuttlefish, and whatever shellfish come to hand, such as mussels or clams, but lacks the saffron.

# *raie au beurre noir*

## SKATE *with* BLACK BUTTER

The nutty bitterness of the sharp little sauce perfectly complements the soft white strands of the skate meat which lie on the gelatinous bones and can be lifted off the skeleton like ribbons. It is a wonderful combination of texture, color, and flavor. Skate is the only fish that needs to be eaten two or three days after it has been caught, by which time the flesh will have ridden itself of the flavor of ammonia, a result of its natural response to stress.

Serves 4

**2lb skate wings**
**1 tablespoon white wine vinegar**

BLACK BUTTER
**1 stick sweet butter**
**4 tablespoons chopped parsley**
**1 tablespoon red wine vinegar**
**salt and freshly milled pepper**

1 Bring the skate wings to the boil in plenty of well-salted water with the white wine vinegar added. Simmer for 10 minutes, remove and drain.

2 Meanwhile, melt the butter in a small skillet. Add the parsley. As soon as the parsley and the butter turn the color of mahogany, lift the pan from the heat. Count to ten and then stir in the red wine vinegar. Without this pause, the hot butter would spurt out of the pan as soon as the vinegar comes in contact with it. Season with a little salt and freshly milled pepper.

3 Arrange the skate wings, dark side uppermost, on a warm serving dish and lift off the dark skin. The flesh slips easily from the soft transparent bones. Sauce with the black butter.

# sole dieppoise

## SOLE *with* CREAM AND SHRIMP

The channel port of Dieppe has an in-shore fleet landing fish from the coasts of Picardy and Normandy. People drive over from Paris to meet the boats, competing with locals, scooping up the catch of shrimp and flat fish. Plaice or lemon sole can replace the sole, as long as they are perfectly fresh.

Serves 4

4 sole (2 if large), filleted and skinned
2 tablespoons all-purpose flour, seasoned
½ stick sweet butter
about 1 cup white wine
1 cup heavy cream
1 tablespoon Pernod (optional)
salt and freshly milled white pepper
4oz raw shrimp, peeled or not

1 Flip the fish fillets in the seasoned flour to apply a light dusting, no more.

2 Melt half the butter in a large skillet. When it foams, lay one or two fish fillets in the pan (or as many as fit without overlapping) and cook until opaque and firm, turning once, allowing 2–3 minutes on each side. Transfer to a warm plate or plates and keep hot while cooking the remaining fish.

3 Add the wine to the buttery residue in the pan and bubble up, scraping off any brown fishy bits. Bubble fiercely until the steam no longer smells of alcohol, and then whisk in the cream and remaining butter, cut into little pieces. Whisk in the Pernod (if using). Taste and season.

4 Slip in the shrimp and reheat gently. Do not let the sauce boil. The crustaceans will cook in a couple of minutes. Pour the sauce over the fish and finish with the shrimp.

**SERVING SUGGESTION** ~ As a main course, serve the sole in the French style, with vegetable accompaniments set on the table for people to help themselves. Plain white rice and braised fennel (see page 105) would be the perfect choice.

**NOTE** ~ Dover sole is skinned first and filleted afterwards, lemon sole should be filleted first, after which the fillets can easily be slipped off their skin with a sharp knife.

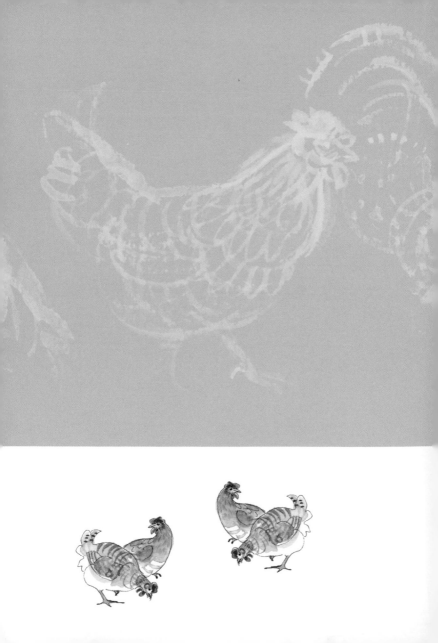

*poultry*

# poulet au beurre

## BUTTER-ROAST CHICKEN

Choose an organic free-range bird for this simple but perfect way with the Sunday chicken. French cooks value flavor and texture over size and plumpness in their poultry, enthusiastically discussing provenance and virtues of each breed, weighing up the merits of the blue-legged chickens of Bresse against those of the succulent chickens of the Landes. In this recipe, a protective coating of herb butter between the skin and the breast keeps the white meat perfectly moist, while the bird is regularly turned to ensure a crisp, buttery skin.

Serves 4–6

**4–5lb chicken with giblets**
**sea salt and freshly milled black pepper**
**1 unwaxed lemon**
**2–3 fresh thyme sprigs**
**6 tablespoons sweet butter**
**3 tablespoons finely chopped fresh tarragon**

1 Preheat the oven to 425°F. Wipe the chicken inside and out and season the cavity generously with salt and pepper. Soften the lemon by rolling it back and forth on a flat surface, and prick it all over with a fork. Tuck the giblets, lemon, and thyme in the cavity.

2 Mash 4 tablespoons of the butter with the tarragon and ½ teaspoon each of salt and pepper. Starting at the neck end of the chicken, work your fingers over one side of the breast between the flesh and skin—be gentle as the skin is fragile. Repeat down the other side.

3 Working on the outside, press the skin to even out the butter, patting the skin back into place. Spread the remaining butter over the chicken, and season.

4 Settle the bird on its side on a rack in a roasting pan. Roast for 20 minutes. Turn it carefully, taking care not to break the skin, and roast on the other side for another 20 minutes. Turn the chicken on to its back, breast up, and roast for another 20 minutes, until the bird is deeply bronzed all over.

5 Reduce the heat to 375°F and turn the chicken breast-side down—try to set it at an angle such that the tail is in the air. Roast for about another 15 minutes, until the juices from the thigh run clear when the meat is pierced with a skewer. No need to baste.

6 Transfer the bird to a warm serving dish, still with its tail in the air, and cover loosely with foil. Let it rest in a turned-off oven (leave the door ajar) for at least 10 minutes—30 minutes is fine. The bird will continue to cook while the meat firms up and the juices are re-absorbed.

7 Carve the chicken in the kitchen and dish it up in its glory. The French never carve at table. Hand around a bowl of undressed salad leaves, such as chicory, mache, and watercress; the buttery juices are the only dressing needed.

# *poulet au riz*

This is a delicate dish that depends on long gentle cooking. A roasting fowl will do, though the broth will be stronger if the bird is an elderly barnyard hen, and the head, neck, and feet (scalded and scrubbed) are included.

∽

Serves 4–6

1 free-range chicken, about 4–5lb, or a mature boiling fowl
2–3 carrots, cut into chunks
3–4 celery sticks, chopped
1 onion, stuck with 2 cloves
a small bunch of parsley, marjoram, thyme, and a bay leaf
finely grated zest and juice of 1 lemon
½ teaspoon white peppercorns
4 cups veal or chicken stock
1 heaped cup round-grain rice
1 stick sweet butter
1 tablespoon all-purpose flour
finely grated zest and juice of ½ lemon
¼ teaspoon grated nutmeg
⅔ cup heavy cream
1 heaped tablespoon finely chopped parsley
salt and freshly milled pepper

1 Wipe the bird inside and out. Place it in a roomy pot, pack the sides with the carrots, celery, onion, herbs, half the lemon zest and juice, peppercorns, and salt. Add the stock and enough water to submerge the ingredients completely.

2 Bring to the boil, cover the pot, and turn down the heat so that the stock simmers. Leave the chicken to cook gently for 1½–2 hours, without allowing any large bubbles to break the surface, until the bird is perfectly tender. If you are using a boiling fowl, allow 2½–3 hours.

2 Rinse the rice in a sieve or fine colander under the cold tap until the water runs clear, then transfer to a pan. Add enough cold water to cover generously, bring to the boil, and cook for 5 minutes, stirring to avoid sticking. Tip the rice back into the sieve or colander and rinse under warm water to wash away the stickiness of the starch.

3 Return the rice to the pan and add 2½ cups of the hot chicken broth from the pot. Bring the rice to the boil, add 2 tablespoons of the butter, turn down the heat, and cook gently for 15–18 minutes, until the grains are perfectly tender. Fork over the rice and add another knob of the butter—the grains should be separate but not dry.

4 Meanwhile make the sauce. Melt another 2 tablespoons of the butter in a small pan. As soon as it foams, sprinkle in the flour, cook very gently for 3–4 minutes until the mixture looks sandy but do not let it brown. Whisk in 2½ cups of the hot chicken broth, bubble up, turn down the heat and simmer gently for 10 minutes.

5 Season the sauce with 1 tablespoon of the remaining lemon juice, a pinch of the finely grated zest and the nutmeg. Bubble up again and whisk over the heat until reduced by a third. Stir in the cream and the remaining butter cut into small pieces and reheat, whisking throughout, until boiling. Taste and add salt and pepper if needed.

6 To serve, heap the rice on an oval serving dish and top with the chicken, skinned and jointed. Finish with a ladleful of the sauce and a shower of finely chopped parsley. Hand the rest of the sauce separately.

**VARIATIONS** ~ For poulet en demi-deuil, literally chicken in half-mourning, slip thin slices of fresh black truffle between the skin and the flesh of the chicken (for perfection, the bird should be entirely covered in truffle) and poach as in the main recipe.

# coq au vin

## CHICKEN IN RED WINE

*A*n ancient recipe from the Auvergne, this is traditionally made with a sinewy barnyard cockerel simmered in the robust red wine of the region—a Chambertin or Macon. A rooster is a lean, muscular bird that needs long gentle cooking to tenderize it. A roasting fowl will only need an hour.

❦

### Serves 4

1 free-range chicken, 4–5lb, jointed, with the back and giblets
salt and freshly milled pepper
1 tablespoon sweet butter
½ cup diced fatty bacon
1lb small shallots or baby onions, peeled but whole
3 cups morels or button mushrooms
2 tablespoons brandy or marc
1 garlic clove, crushed with a little salt
1 bottle robust red wine
a small bunch of bay, parsley, and thyme

#### BEURRE MANIE
1 tablespoon sweet butter
1 tablespoon all-purpose flour

1 Trim the chicken joints of any excess fat, but do not skin them. Season with salt and pepper and set aside.

2 Melt half the butter in a roomy casserole and fry the bacon and shallots or onions until lightly browned, then remove and reserve. Add the morels or button mushrooms, sprinkle with a little salt, and let them fry in the hot juices for a few minutes, then remove and add them to the reserved onions.

3 Melt the remaining butter in the pot and add the chicken joints. Fry them until they take a little color, then sprinkle with the brandy and set it alight to burn off the alcohol and caramelize the chicken skin a little.

4 Add the garlic and red wine, and bubble up. Return the reserved onions, bacon, and mushrooms to the pot, season with salt and pepper, and tuck in the herbs. Bring back to the boil, turn down the heat, and cover tightly. Leave to simmer gently for 1–1½ hours, until the chicken is perfectly tender.

5 Work the butter to a smooth paste with the flour to make the beurre manié. Remove the herbs and transfer the chicken joints to a warm serving dish with the mushrooms and onions. Return the pot to the heat, bubble up the juices, and whisk in the beurre manié. Bubble the sauce up for a few minutes until it is smooth, glossy, and no longer tastes of raw flour.

6 Pour the sauce over the chicken. Serve with potatoes mashed with hot milk and sweet butter, or country-style, with thick slices of country bread for mopping the juices. Accompany with the same robust red wine that served as the cooking broth.

# suprême de volaille aux morilles

### BREAST OF CHICKEN *with* MOREL MUSHROOMS

The tender white breast meat on a chicken is known as the suprême, one on each side of the breast bone. A French cook would expect to buy the whole bird and have the butcher prepare the suprêmes as required—skinned or not, with or without a hank of wing-bone. The carcasses would then provide the basis for a fine strong stock, the meat picked from the bones and folded into a béchamel sauce as the filling for a vol-au-vent ordered from the pâtisserie.

Serves 4

**4 chicken breasts**
**2 tablespoons all-purpose flour, seasoned**
**1½ cups fresh morels or 1 cup dried and soaked morels**
**½ stick sweet butter**
**1 cup white wine**
**about ½ cup heavy cream**
**pinch of sugar (optional)**
**salt and freshly milled pepper**

1 Wipe the chicken breasts and flip them over in the seasoned flour. Carefully clean the fresh morels: do not rinse the caps but use a brush to get the sand out of the wrinkles; trim the bases as they are inclined to be woody. Drain soaked dried morels and reserve the soaking liquid.

2 Melt the butter in a roomy skillet. As soon as it foams, lay the chicken breasts in the pan. Fry gently, turning once, for 5 minutes or so, until the meat begins to firm up.

3 Add the morels (if soaked, include the reserved soaking water) and wine and bubble up. Turn down the heat, cover the pan loosely, and simmer gently for 10–15 minutes, until the alcohol has evaporated and the breasts are firm.

4 Remove the lid and bubble up to reduce the juices to a couple of spoonfuls. Stir in the cream and check the seasoning (adding a little sugar, perhaps). Bubble up again to amalgamate the cream with the wine sauce. Transfer everything to a warm serving dish. Simple, really.

**NOTE** ~ The chicken is good with a puree of celery root and potato spiced with a little nutmeg.

Other wild mushrooms can replace the morels: chanterelles, pieds de mouton, trompettes de la mort; cultivated oyster mushrooms and button mushrooms are also suitable.

# chaud-froid de poulet

## POACHED CHICKEN SALAD

An exquisite dish whose excellence depends on perfect raw materials. A free-range chicken is poached, allowed to cool in its own juices, and then dressed with home-made lemon mayonnaise enriched with a reduction of the cooking broth. There is absolutely no need for fancy garnishings—just let the flavor of the dish tell its own story.

Serves 4–6

1 small free-range chicken
1 small onion, quartered
2–3 celery tops
1 leek, cut into chunks
1 teaspoon allspice berries
½ teaspoon white peppercorns
1 teaspoon salt

MAYONNAISE
2 egg yolks
finely grated zest and juice of 1 lemon
1 teaspoon mild French mustard (tarragon mustard is good)
scant 2 cups light olive oil or half olive oil
and half sunflower oil
salt and freshly milled white pepper

TO SERVE
crisp hot bread rolls
quartered lettuce hearts
tomato salad

❧

1 Remove any extraneous fat from inside the chicken. Settle the bird, breast uppermost, in a roomy pot that will just accommodate it, and pour in enough cold water to submerge it completely. Bring to the boil and skim off any gray foam that rises to the surface.

2 Add the onion, celery tops, leek, allspice, peppercorns, and salt. Bring back to the boil, turn down the heat so that the water simmers gently and cover the pan. Poach the chicken delicately for about 1 hour without letting it boil, adding more hot water if necessary. The French say the liquid should smile. If you prefer, transfer the pan to the oven once the liquid has boiled, and leave it to simmer at 325°F. The chicken is done when the thigh waggles easily in the socket.

3 Let the chicken cool for 30 minutes in its cooking broth. Remove, skin, and strip all the meat from the bones; do not forget the little oysters (two small round nuggets of meat) from the back. Transfer the meat to a bowl, pour in a couple of ladlefuls of broth and place in the fridge for the chicken to drink its juices—overnight is best, but 4–5 hours will do. Reserve the broth and keep it in the fridge.

4 Remove the chicken pieces from their jelly and cut them into bite-sized strips—the meat will be deliciously moist and gelatinous. Carefully lift off the hat of set white fat on the excess jelly and the reserved jellied broth (it is lovely for frying potatoes) and tip both into a pan. Boil the broth down until it is reduced to a scant cup).

5 Leave the broth to cool while you make the mayonnaise. When you begin, all ingredients should be at room temperature. Put the egg yolks in a bowl and add 1 teaspoon of the lemon juice and the mustard. Blend quickly with a wire whisk, then whisk in the oil, adding it very slowly at first. Steadily increase the stream of oil as it is incorporated and the mayonnaise thickens, working in more lemon juice—not too much, just enough to sharpen the mayonnaise.

6 As soon as the mayonnaise starts to thicken it is easier to switch to a wooden spoon. You may need more or less oil, depending on the weather and the size of the yolks, but the mixture should be about the consistency of soft butter. Beat in enough of the cooled chicken stock to dilute the mayonnaise to a coating consistency. Stir in the lemon zest, taste, and season.

7 Combine the shredded chicken with the mayonnaise and serve with hot crisp rolls, quartered lettuce hearts, and a little salad of chopped peeled tomatoes dressed with a pinch of sugar.

# pintade farcie aux pommes

## STUFFED GUINEA FOWL *with* APPLES

This sumptuous party dish comes from Normandy, land of Calvados and cream. The apples in the stuffing impart a flowery fragrance to the gamey little guinea fowl, while the gentle braising keeps them juicy. Guinea fowl, an African native, is comparatively recently domesticated and, although it is a popular barnyard bird in rural France, it has retained the muscular leanness of its wild ancestor. Four partridges, a brace of pheasant, or 2 small free-range chickens are the alternatives.

Serves 6

**2 guinea fowl**
**1 onion, finely chopped**
**¼ cup butter**
**6oz ground pork**
**4oz ground beef**
**6 yellow-fleshed apples, such as Reinettes or Golden Delicious**
**1 small glass Calvados or brandy**
**1 egg, forked to blend**
**salt and pepper**
**1 teaspoon dried thyme**

TO FINISH
**6 tablespoons créme fraîche or heavy cream soured with a little
lemon juice**
**1 tablespoon butter for frying**

1 Preheat the oven to 400°F. Wipe the birds inside and out,
and singe off any stray little hairs or feathers by turning
them quickly over a gas flame. (Or use long matches to singe
off the hairs.)

2 For the stuffing, fry the onion in half the butter. Add the pork
and beef, and fry gently until the meats have changed color.

3 Peel and dice 2 of the apples, and add them to the pan.
Sprinkle with the Calvados or brandy and cover loosely.
Leave to stew gently for 15–20 minutes, until the apple pieces
have softened but have not quite lost their shape. Season with salt

and pepper, remove from the heat and let the mixture cool a little before you work in the egg.

4 Divide the stuffing between the birds, spooning it into their body cavities. Tie their drumsticks together with thread to keep them neatly in shape. Transfer the stuffed birds to a roasting pan, breasts downwards. Dot with the remaining butter, add a sprinkle of thyme, and salt and pepper.

5 Roast the birds at the high heat for the first 10 minutes. Turn the birds breast side up, dot with a little more butter, and cover with foil, shiny side down. Reduce the heat to 300°F so that the birds cook slowly and make plenty of juice. Cook for about 1 hour, until the birds are perfectly tender and the drumsticks pull easily away from the body.

6 Remove from the oven and leave to rest for 10 minutes. Quarter the birds and pile the stuffing up in the middle of a warm serving dish. Tip the pan juices into a small pan, skim off the oily slick of butter from the top and reserve.

7 Reheat the juices and bubble up fiercely for 3–4 minutes to reduce them to a strong sticky gravy. Stir in the créme fraîche or cream, taste, season, and reheat without boiling.

8 Meanwhile peel, quarter, and core the remaining apples and sauté in the reserved butter until lightly browned, taking care they do not lose their shape (you may need extra butter).

9 Arrange the apple quarters on the stuffing and pile the quartered birds on top. Trickle with a little of the sauce and hand the rest of the sauce separately.

# caneton à la bigarade

## DUCKLING *with* ORANGE

A dish for winter, when the ducklings are well grown and bitter oranges, bigarades—otherwise known as marmalade or Seville oranges—are in season. Choose unwaxed fruit or scrub them thoroughly to remove the coating. A duck carcass weighs heavy and the meat to bone ratio is not as favorable as it is with other birds, so allow 1lb 5oz per person.

Serves 4

1 well-grown duckling, about 4–5lb dressed weight
2 tablespoons sweet butter
salt and freshly milled pepper

### TO FINISH
3 bitter oranges or 2 sweet oranges plus the juice of 1 lemon
1 heaped tablespoon superfine sugar
2 tablespoons chicken or veal stock
¼ cup butter, chilled and chopped small

1 Preheat the oven to 325°F. Rub the duckling inside and out with salt and pepper and truss it neatly. Melt the butter in a heavy flameproof casserole, add the bird and brown it all over.

2 Cover tightly and cook in the oven for 25–30 minutes. Alternatively, cook over low heat, turning the bird regularly to avoid burning. Remove from the heat when the juices spooned from the cavity are a clear pink—a duck should always be slightly undercooked and the breast meat should be rosy rather than gray or the bird will be tough.

3 Meanwhile, finely pare the zest from the oranges and cut it into fine strips or use a zester to remove the zest in strands. Pare and discard the pith from the flesh and carve out the segments, leaving the membranes behind and squeezing the juice from them into a bowl. Reserve the zest, juice, and segments (discard the pips).

4 When the duck is perfectly roasted, transfer it to a hot serving dish and surround with the orange segments. Pour off the excess fat from the casserole, then reserve the cooking juices in the casserole, setting it aside.

5 Place the sugar in a small, heavy-based pan and heat gently until it melts and caramelizes lightly—you are looking for a pale golden brown. Add the lemon juice (if using) and remove from the heat. Stir in the stock and the reserved orange zest and juice, return to the heat and bubble up.

6 Add the orange mixture to the drippings in the pan and bubble up again, scraping the base to include all the sticky

brown bits. Strain the sauce, taste, and season. Reheat to boiling
and whisk in the butter to thicken the sauce and give it a shine.

7 Carve the duck before you take it to table, and coat the
portions with the sauce.

**VARIATIONS** ~ For caneton au navets, duck with turnips,
prepare the duckling as above, omitting the oranges, and serve
with baby turnips caramelized in butter with a little sugar and
finished in the duck juices.

For caneton au petits pois, duck with peas, prepare the duck
as above, omitting the oranges. Cook freshly shelled peas in
the duck juices; finish with nuggets of chilled butter to add
thickness and shine.

For caneton aux olives, duck with olives, cook the duck as
above, omitting the oranges. Finish the juices with green olives
(scald them first to remove excess salt) and a few flakes of
chilled butter.

# magrets de canard poêlés

## SEARED DUCK BREASTS

The simplest way to ensure that the choicest morsel of the bird, the breast meat, remains tender and juicy is to cook it very briefly over a high heat, and then let it rest and firm up. The French have a choice of two breeds of domestic duck. The Nantais—named for the town of Nantes—is the smaller and weighs around 3¼lb, while the Rouennais—after the town of Rouen—weighs well over 4½lb. The Rouennais is not bled during slaughter, a method that produces much darker meat which, though delicious when cooked rare and pink, is more vulnerable to spoilage. Buy the whole duck, lift the breasts off the bone with a sharp knife, and make a pâté with the carcass and legs.

～

### Serves 2

**2 duck breasts, boned**
**salt and freshly milled pepper**

1 Lightly score the duck skin without cutting through to the flesh. Season the meat on both sides.

2 Heat a heavy iron pan until smoking. Place the duck breasts skin sides down on the hot metal and cook for 3–4 minutes, until the fat softens and begins to run, and the skin gilds.

3 Turn the duck breasts carefully and sear them on the other side, allowing another 2–3 minutes. Remove the pan from the heat and leave on the side of the stove for 5 minutes for the meat to firm up and settle. Test for doneness by prodding with your index finger: very rare meat feels soft and spongy; if the meat feels hard, it's overdone (unlikely at this point). If the duck breasts are still soft, set the oven at 325°F and transfer them to the oven for 10 minutes. Duck breast should be quite pink, almost bloody. To serve, slice them on the diagonal.

**SERVING SUGGESTIONS** ~ Serve with pommes de terre salardaises (see page 96). Alternatively, boil potatoes, slice them while they are still hot and sauté them in goose fat. They are ready when they are golden brown and flecked with little crisp bits. For absolute perfection, include a few slivers of black Périgord truffle.

You can, if you wish, make a little sauce to go with the duck. Deglaze the pan with a splash of Armagnac and stir in some cream or boil up a glass of red wine with the pan drippings and finish with a knob of cold butter.

# garbure béarnaise

## SLOW-COOKED VEGETABLES *with* GOOSE CONFIT

The garbure, the traditional rural midday meal of southern France, is at its most sumptuous in the kitchens of Béarn. At its simplest, it is a meatless vegetarian hot-pot much like Italy's minestrone. But in Béarn it always includes a joint or two of confit, fattened goose or duck preserved in its own dripping. Traditionally, it was sent to the breadmaker's oven, a service once provided by the village baker. The basic ingredients are variable, depending on season and regional preference: in Provence, a ratatouille layer is usual; in the Languedoc in spring, green vegetables and potatoes replace the beans and cabbage. You can replace the confit with pork chops or omit the meat altogether.

Serves 4 as a main dish

**8 thick slices country bread**
**1lb onions**
**8 tablespoons olive oil**
**1–2 bay leaves**
**4 tablespoons chopped mixed parsley, chervil, and marjoram**
**2–3 garlic cloves, chopped**
**salt and freshly milled pepper**
**4–5 large tomatoes, peeled and chopped**
**4 tablespoons cooked navy beans**
**2 leg joints of goose or duck confit (see page 181)**
**1 large chunk pumpkin or butternut squash, peeled and sliced**
**½ green cabbage, shredded**
**grated cheese to finish (optional)**

TO SERVE
**green salad**
**pickled gherkins and capers**

1 Preheat the oven to 325°F. Slice the bread and put it to dry and crisp for 10 minutes or so while the oven heats up.

2 Meanwhile, fry the onions gently in 3 tablespoons of the olive oil until soft and golden—do not let them brown further.

3 Now you are ready to assemble the garbure. Spread half the onion in a layer in the base of a roomy casserole. Top with half the dried bread. Season with bay, chopped herbs, garlic, and salt and pepper. Top with layers of tomatoes, beans, confit,

pumpkin, and a handful of the shredded cabbage, seasoning between the layers each time.

4 Repeat the layering in the same order, finishing with the remaining bread. Pour in a tumbler of water and trickle with the rest of the oil.

5 Cover tightly and bake for about 1½–2 hours, until everything is deliciously tender. Turn the oven down a notch after the first hour and check if you need to add a little more water. Take the cover off for the last 15 minutes, sprinkle with a thick layer of grated cheese (if using), and turn the oven up to crisp the top.

6 To serve, scoop through the layers and ladle the garbure into deep soup plates. Offer a green salad and pickles (gherkins, capers) on the side. You will need a carafe of red wine for the goudale—the term for a glass of wine poured into the last of the broth and drunk straight from the plate. Very rustic.

*Cuisine is when things taste
like themselves....In cooking,
as in all the arts, simplicity
is the sign of perfection.*

**Curnonsky,** French gourmet (1872–1956)

# cassoulet de castelnaudary

## BEANS BAKED *with* GOOSE CONFIT

The cassoulet of Castelnaudary, according to the inhabitants of the windswept town in the Languedoc where my children attended school, is the only true version of this stupendous bean pot. And who am I argue? In Toulouse or Carcassonne, they might add mutton or lamb, some might even include a brace of partridges, but Madame Escrieux (my neighbour, whose recipe this is) would have none of these. The Escrieux family, subsistence farmers with the right to operate their own still, potted their own confit, grew their own beans (though the beans of Soissons were held acceptable), and kept and slaughtered their own pig. The dish was reserved for the winter months and only eaten at midday on Sunday, since it needed a full day and a night to digest.

Serves 6–8

FIRST COOKING

**2lb white navy beans**
**1 whole head garlic**
**1lb belly pork, tied in a roll**
**2 large carrots, cut into chunks**
**1 onion, stuck with 6 cloves**
**a small bunch of bay, parsley, thyme, and rosemary**
**½ teaspoon cracked black pepper**

SECOND COOKING

**1–2 joints of goose or duck confit (see page 181)**
**1lb lean pork, cut into bite-sized chunks**
**3 garlic cloves, crushed**
**1 onion, chopped**
**1lb tomatoes, peeled and chopped (canned are fine)**
**1lb fresh all-meat pork sausage, such as saucisson de Toulouse**
**4 tablespoons goose fat from the confit, melted**
**salt and freshly milled pepper**

TO FINISH

**2–3 tablespoons fresh bread crumbs**

∽

1 Soak the beans overnight in cold water. Drain and transfer to a large cooking pot—a toupin is the correct container. For a charred, lightly caramelized flavor, turn the head of garlic over in a gas flame.

2 Remove the skin from the belly pork and tie it up in a neat roll; dice the pork. Add the meat and roll of skin to the beans in the pot with all the other ingredients for the first cooking: the garlic, carrots, onion, herbs, and pepper. Cover all the ingredients generously with fresh water, bring to the boil, and skim off the grey foam which rises. Boil for 10 minutes. Then turn down the heat and simmer the beans for 1 hour, or until they are soft but still whole, adding more boiling water if necessary.

3 Meanwhile, prepare the ingredients for the second cooking. Warm the joints of goose or duck confit in a roomy frying pan until the fat runs, then remove and reserve the meat. Fry the pork with the garlic in the drippings, until all the pieces are browned. Remove and reserve both meat and garlic. Fry the onion in the drippings until soft and golden.

4 Preheat the oven to 300°F. When the beans are ready, take out the garlic, onion, and the herbs. Remove and untie the roll of belly pork and lay it in the base of a roomy casserole, fat downwards. Drain the beans, reserving the cooking liquor. Layer half the beans in the casserole with the meats, onions, tomatoes, and sausage. Finish with the rest of the beans. Pour in the reserved cooking liquor to cover the ingredients. Cover the pot.

5 Transfer to the oven and leave to cook gently for about 2 hours. If the beans get too dry, pour in a little boiling water (the beans will harden if you use cold water).

6 Trickle a tablespoonful of the melted goose fat over the beans. Increase the oven heat to 325°F and return the pot, uncovered, to the oven. It will take 30 minutes to form a beautiful crust. Break it with a spoon and stir it into the beans

once more. Sprinkle with the bread crumbs and trickle with another tablespoonful of goose fat.

7 Return the casserole to the oven for 30 minutes, then break the crust again and stir it in. Trickle with the remaining goose fat. Leave for the final 30 minutes. Now you reap the reward of your patience: beneath the golden crust the meats will be tender and fragrant, and the beans melted into a delicious creamy mass.

**MAKING DUCK OR GOOSE CONFIT** ~ To make your own confit, choose a large pottery or stoneware ovenproof jar or pot and drop in as many duck or goose joints as will comfortably fit. Season with salt, peppercorns, a bay leaf, and juniper berries. Melt the contents of a tin of gras d'oie (available from the supermarket deli section) and pour in enough to completely submerge the duck joints. Heat the oven to the lowest possible setting and leave the duck or goose in the oven overnight. That's all.

To use, melt gently and remove the joints. The confit is delicious as the star ingredient of a warm salad; the fat makes exquisitely crisp sauté potatoes that are terrific with a few wild mushrooms, maybe the first of the year's chanterelles.

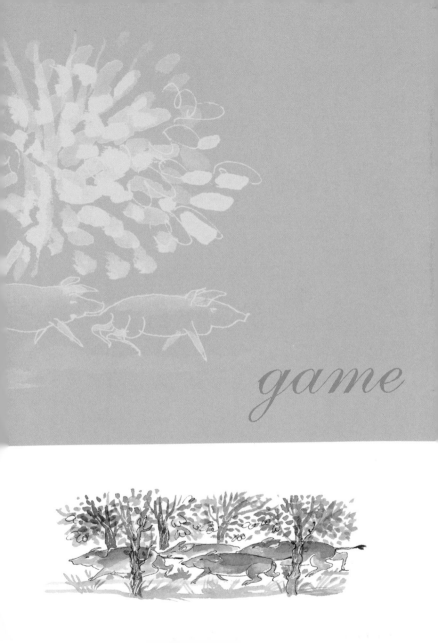

*game*

# *marcassin en daube*

## SLOW-COOKED WILD BOAR

To flavor a daube, the cooks of Provence like to use dried orange zest, and the common variety of thyme is replaced by serpolet, a highly aromatic wild member of the same family. The daubière is the closed earthenware pot in which stews are traditionally simmered.

Serves 6

4lb wild boar meat, diced
2 tablespoons all-purpose flour, seasoned
4–5 tablespoons olive oil
8 garlic cloves, in their skins
2 tablespoons diced streaky bacon
3 large tomatoes, peeled and chopped
1–2 sprigs serpolet or thyme
1 curl orange zest, preferably dried, but fresh is fine
1 glass white wine
2½ cups stock

TO FINISH
1 cup mushrooms, chopped
1 tablespoon olive oil
4 salted anchovies
½ cup black olives, chopped
salt and freshly milled pepper

1 Dust the meat in the seasoned flour and fry in the olive oil until it browns a little. Wild meat is drier and firmer than farmed meat, so it takes less time to caramelize. Remove from the pan and reserve.

2 Add the whole unskinned garlic cloves and the bacon to the pan drippings and fry for a few minutes. Add the tomatoes, serpolet or thyme and orange zest and bubble up, squashing the tomatoes down until they collapse.

3 Pour in the wine and the stock and bubble up again. Return the meat to the pan and add seasoning. Turn down the heat, cover the pan loosely and leave to simmer gently, for as long as it takes for the meat to be so tender it can be eaten with a fork— about 2–3 hours—add a little water if necessary.

4 When the meat is nearly done, fry the mushrooms in the oil in a small skillet. Add the anchovies and mash them into the mushrooms so they melt in the hot juices. Add the olives and heat for 1–2 minutes. Stir this aromatic mixture into the stew 5 minutes before the end of cooking.

**SERVING SUGGESTION** ~ Serve with white rice or fresh noodles, lightly buttered, and rough country bread rubbed with garlic.

Wild boar, marcassin, is the most prized of the huntsman's bag and is still to be found in the mountainous and forested areas of France where cultivation is impractical or which were formerly reserved as the king's hunting forest. Following the implementation of the Code Napoleon (the basis of French laws, particularly those of inheritance) possessions had to be divided equally among all recognized heirs, reversing the law of inheritance by first born and turning France into a nation of small farmers. The result was that most land fell into the hands of subsistence farmers. These days even the most urban French citizen considers himself a countryman, possessed of a stake in a patch of scrub which, however small, can be viewed as his personal hunting territory; a change from the days when the produce of the king's hunting forest was reserved for the royal table.

Wild meat is noticeably leaner, darker and more sinewy than the domesticated equivalent; it takes best to long slow cooking in a daube or as the basis for a country pâté. Recipes for wild meat usually include additional fat, for example from belly pork or bacon, to counter the natural leanness and help to tenderize the meat, rather than allowing it to remain chewy. Wine, particularly when used as a marinade, enhances the gamey flavor, though the alcohol must always be evaporated during cooking.

Flavoring herbs, particularly rosemary, thyme, oregano, juniper, and wild garlic, are chosen to reflect the diet available in the wild, when they are consumed in the form of young shoots, berries, or roots. When cooking game, a touch of romance—preferably the huntsman's own description of the chase—is as much a part of the recipe as the ingredients.

Even in highly cultivated areas, the Frenchman is so devoted to the possibilities of la chasse that patches of woodland and scrub are left as shelter for small game—hare, rabbits, partridge, pheasant—and as gathering patches for wild fungi and fruits.

Although a boar is the most prized of the hunter's bag —a quarry admired as much for the danger of the pursuit as for the excellence of the meat—venison and hare are also valued, and recipes for one or the other are interchangeable. Rabbit is the poor man's meat, is usually trapped rather than hunted, and is not protected by a closed season. Of the feathered game, quail is no longer available from the wild (the disappearance is blamed on over-enthusiastic netting on the islands of the Mediterranean during the birds' bi-annual migrations), and the small birds—thrushes, ortolans, fig-peckers—are no longer hunted, at least for commercial reasons. Nevertheless, French country-folk don't take kindly to being told what they can and cannot bring home for the pot and hunting is seen as a way of life, a right as well as a pleasure. Among isolated rural communities, it was a way of escaping routine domesticity in more ways than one. A friend and neighbour of mine in the Languedoc told me she always knew when her husband, under pretence of setting traps for rabbits, had visited his fancy woman across the valley because when he returned home, his clothes were perfumed with sarriette, a variety of thyme which only grew on the southern slopes of the hillside, along the path which led to her dwelling.

∽

# civet de lièvre

## SLOW-COOKED HARE *in* RED WINE

Acivet can be made with venison, rabbit, any game birds, or a mixture. Game is lean, dry meat which needs extra fat—petit salé (salt-cured belly pork, or fatty bacon). To prepare your own petit salé, buy a thick slice of fatty belly pork, sprinkle with rough salt, cracked pepper, and bay leaf, and leave overnight.

Serves 8–10

**2 bay leaves**
**1 thyme sprig**
**1 rosemary sprig**
**1 teaspoon dried oregano**
**2 garlic cloves, roughly chopped**
**1 bottle robust red wine**
**1 well–grown hare, trimmed and cut into small joints**
**about 2 tablespoons all-purpose flour**
**4 tablespoons olive oil**
**1lb shallots or pickling onions, skinned**
**2–3 carrots, cut into chunks**
**1 thick slice petit salé or belly pork, salted overnight, diced**
**½ teaspoon grated nutmeg**
**salt and freshly milled pepper**

### TO FINISH
**the hare's blood or 2 squares bitter black chocolate, chopped**

1 Mix the bay leaves, thyme, rosemary, oregano, garlic, and wine in a roomy bowl. Add the hare and turn pieces in the marinade. Cover and leave the meat to absorb the flavors—overnight is best.

2 Drain the hare, reserving the marinade, pat dry and dust with flour. Heat the oil in a large casserole and add the onions, carrots, and petit salé or belly pork. Fry until they caramelize a little and remove. Set aside on a plate.

3 Fry the pieces of hare until lightly browned. Add the reserved marinade and a cupful of water and bubble up. Replace the pork mixture. Turn down the heat, cover tightly, and leave to simmer quietly for 1½–2 hours, until the meat is falling off the bone and the sauce is thick, rich, and dark. Alternatively, the casserole can be transferred to the oven to cook very gently at 275°F. Check occasionally and add a splash of boiling water if the casserole is drying out.

4 Stir in the blood or chocolate and cook gently for 1–2 minutes, stirring until the sauce has accepted the addition. Do not boil or the sauce will curdle. It's good today, even better tomorrow.

# lapin à la moutarde

### RABBIT *with* MUSTARD

*A*lthough wild rabbit has a finer flavor, the hutch rabbits reared in every well-stocked French barnyard are well flavored and guaranteed to be tender. When preparing rabbit for the pot, remember to remove the clear membrane that covers the saddle and hind legs or the meat will never be really tender however long you cook it. Use a sharp knife—you have to be brutal and waste a bit of flesh.

Serves 4

2 wild or 1 tame rabbit, cut into neat pieces
1 tablespoon all-purpose flour, seasoned
4–5 tablespoons oil or melted butter
2 onions, finely chopped
1–2 thyme sprigs
1 glass white wine
2½ cups stock or water
salt and freshly milled pepper

TO FINISH
1 tablespoon mild Dijon mustard
1 tablespoon wholegrain mustard (Meaux)
4 tablespoons créme fraîche or heavy cream
buttered noodles or white rice to serve

1 Pick over the rabbit portions, removing any fluff or sharp splinters of bone. Toss the portions in the flour. Heat the oil or butter in a roomy pan and fry the portions until they seize and brown a little. Remove and reserve.

2 Add the onions to the hot pan juices and fry gently until they soften and gild but do not let them brown further. Return the rabbit to the pan and add the thyme, wine, and water or stock. Bubble up, scraping in any sticky bits from the pan, turn down the heat, season and cover loosely.

3 Leave to simmer gently for as long as it takes for the rabbit to be so tender it can be eaten with a fork. A young animal will be ready in 30–40 minutes, an older rabbit may take over 1 hour.

4 When the rabbit is perfectly tender, stir in the mustard and cream, bubble up again and serve with buttered noodles or plain white rice to soak up the juices.

# pigeonneaux poêles aux bolets

## GRILLED PIGEONS *with* MUSHROOMS

In the days when self-sufficiency was possible, most rural households kept and fattened up a lot of pigeons for the pot. While the young birds (squabs) were tender enough for roasting, this recipe suited elderly birds that had outlived their usefulness as breeders as well as wild birds of uncertain age that fed on the crops. The number of birds to cook depends on appetites. The recipe also works well with fillets from a saddle of hare, or magrets of wild duck (use a sharp knife to lift the breast fillets from the rib cage). A gratin dauphinoise (see page 92) is the perfect accompaniment.

Serves 4

**4–8 pigeons**
**2 tablespoons olive oil**
**1 teaspoon dried thyme**
**salt and freshly milled pepper**
**1 onion, cut into chunks**
**1–2 carrots, cut into chunks**
**1 stick celery, chopped**
**1 small turnip, cut into chunks**
**a small bunch of bay, parsley, and thyme**
**a few peppercorns**
**1 cup dried cep**
**⅔ cup madeira or dessert wine**

TO FINISH
**¾ stick sweet butter, cut into large dice and chilled**
**large bunch of watercress**

ᥴᥱᢣᦱ

1 Use a sharp knife to lift the pigeon breast fillets off their rib cages. Brush with oil, sprinkle with thyme and season with salt and freshly milled pepper. Wrap the breast fillets in plastic wrap and reserve.

2 Roast the carcasses with a little of the oil and onion, carrots, celery, and turnip for 15 minutes in a very hot oven. Transfer the roast mixture to a roomy pan. Add 3¾ cups water and drop in the herbs, a few peppercorns, and a little salt. Bring to the boil, turn down the heat and cover loosely. Simmer gently for 1–2 hours.

3 Meanwhile, put the ceps in a cupful of hot water to soak and swell for 30 minutes. Strain, reserving the ceps, and add the soaking liquid to the pot.

4 Strain the stock, return it to the pot, and add the soaked ceps. Bubble up, turn down the heat, and simmer for about 30 minutes, until the liquid has reduced to ⅔ cup and the ceps are tender. Add the madeira or dessert wine and bubble up fiercely for a moment to evaporate the alcohol, then simmer until reduced to 4 tablespoons of well-flavored sauce.

5 When you are nearly ready to serve, preheat the oven to 275°F and preheat the broiler or heat a heavy skillet. Make sure the fillets are at room temperature. Sear them in the pan or under the broiler using very fierce heat for 60 seconds on each side. Then transfer to the oven and leave for a minimum of 10 minutes and maximum 25 minutes, for the meat to firm and settle, and lose its rawness. Pigeon breasts should be pink and juicy—if overcooked, they will be gray and tough.

6 Just before you are about to serve the pigeons, bring the sauce back to the boil and whisk in the nuggets of cold butter one by one until the sauce thickens and becomes shiny.

7 Slice the pigeon breasts diagonally into pretty pink slices. Transfer to warm plates, sauce generously and serve with a hank of watercress on the side.

"Cookery is not chemistry. It is an art. It requires instinct and taste rather than exact measurements."

**Marcel Boulestin,** chef and food writer (1878–1943)

# cailles aux raisins

### ROAST QUAIL STUFFED *with* GRAPES

R emember *Babette's Feast*, when she tucked the little quails into the vol-au-vent cases? Small birds are always festive and farmed quail are deliciously tender—a real treat. Most people will manage two birds, some can eat three.

Serves 4

8–12 quail
¼ bottle white wine
2 tablespoons olive oil
1 teaspoon crumbled thyme
salt and freshly milled pepper
4oz small white grapes
1 stick sweet butter

TO FINISH
a few small white grapes, skinned and seeds removed
large bunch of watercress

1 Marinate the birds for a few hours (or overnight in the fridge) in the white wine, olive oil, thyme, salt, and pepper.

2 Preheat the oven to 400°F. Remove the birds and pat them dry, reserving the marinade for the sauce. Tuck a whole grape or two and a knob of butter inside each quail. Mash the remaining butter with salt and pepper and rub it over the breasts. Place in a roasting pan.

3 Roast the birds for 20–30 minutes, until the little legs move easily in their joints. Remove the quail from the pan and reserve, covered loosely with foil, while you make the sauce.

4 Set the roasting pan on the heat and pour in the marinade. Bubble it up, scraping in all the sticky brown drippings. Cook until the alcohol has evaporated and the sauce looks glossy. Taste, season, and stir in the finishing grapes.

5 Serve the roasted birds on a bed of watercress and hand out the sauce separately.

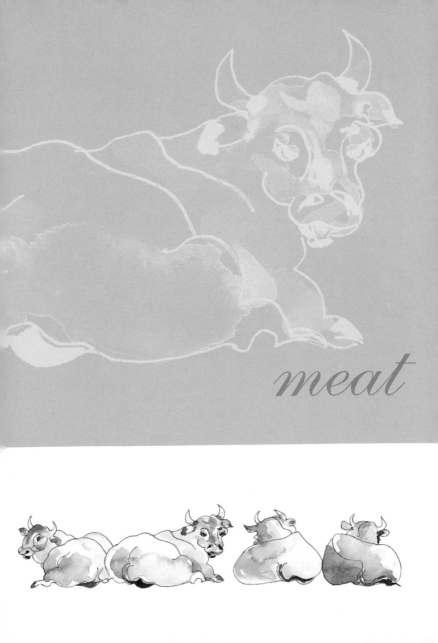

*meat*

# pot-au-feu

## POT-SIMMERED BEEF

*I learned how to prepare the classic Sunday boiled dinner from my neighbors, subsistence farmers in the Languedoc, when my children attended school in Castelnaudary. Beef was considered a luxury since it had to be bought from the butcher. The three different cuts of meat were so important that the dish would not be made if one of them was lacking. The rib or skirt is for flavor, the shin for strength, and the knuckle or marrow bone, or oxtail, for richness.*

### Serves 6–8

2lb boneless rib of beef, flank or skirt, tied with string
1lb shin of beef, tied with string
1 knuckle or marrow bone or oxtail, cut into chunks
3–4 large carrots, cut into chunks (save the trimmings)
2–3 large leeks, cut into chunks (save the trimmings)
2 onions, unskinned and quartered
½ teaspoon peppercorns
1–2 bay leaves
salt
1 head celery, preferably green, cut into chunks
2 small turnips, cut into chunks (save the trimmings)
1lb potatoes
½ small green cabbage, cut into wedges

1 Put the beef and bones in a large stew pan or earthenware casserole. Cover with 8 cups cold water. Bring to the boil and skim off the foam.

2 Add the trimmings from the carrots and leeks, the onions, peppercorns, bay leaves, and 1 teaspoon salt. Bring the water back to the boil, allow it to give one big belch and then turn down the heat. Simmer gently for 3 hours, by which time the meat should be tender.

3 Strain the broth, discarding the trimmings and the onion. Either return the meat to the broth and leave it to cool overnight, then lift off the solid layer of fat before you reheat the broth, or skim off the fat with a spoon while the broth is still hot, then return the meat to the broth.

4 Reheat the meat and broth and add the carrots, leeks, celery, and turnips. Bring back to the boil, turn down the heat and simmer for 10 minutes. Add the potatoes, reheat to boiling, turn down the heat and simmer for another 10 minutes. Add the cabbage wedges and bring back to the boil. Simmer for 10 minutes more, until all the vegetables are tender.

5 Slice the meat into manageable pieces and arrange with the vegetables in a large warm serving dish. Serve moistened with a ladleful of stock, handing more separately as a sauce. Accompany with a bunch of small red radishes, rinsed but still with their leaves; salt-cured capers, well-rinsed and dressed with wine vinegar; and cornichons (very small pickled gherkins).

# daube de bœuf

## SLOW-COOKED BEEF *with* WINE AND OLIVES

**T**his is one of those slow-simmered winter stews, farmhouse fare, which takes its name from the pot in which it's cooked. The composition varies: this particular version comes from the olive-town of Nyons in Haute Provence. Dried orange zest adds a subtle hint of summer. To prepare your own, simply pare the zest from an orange, dry it on a window sill and store.

Serves 4–6

2lb stewing beef, trimmed
8oz belly pork, diced
2 tablespoons pork lard or olive oil
1 onion, chopped
1 large carrot, diced
1 celery stick, diced
4 garlic cloves, crushed
1lb small shallots or pickling onions, peeled
2–3 tablespoons white brandy
1 tablespoon black olives (the wrinkly salted little olives of Nyons are perfect)
1–2 curls dried orange zest
1 short cinnamon stick
1–2 bay leaves
1 cup strong red wine
salt and freshly milled pepper

1 Have ready a large round-bellied earthenware casserole or whichever pot you use to cook a stew. Cut the beef into bite-sized pieces. Remove the skin from the belly pork, then dice the meat and cut the skin into small squares.

2 Heat the lard or oil in a roomy skillet and add the onion, carrot, celery, and garlic. Fry them for a moment, then push them aside and add the shallots or baby onions. Fry gently until they take a little color.

3 Push the vegetables aside, add the meat and let it brown a little. Sprinkle with the marc or eau de vie and light it with a match to burn off the alcohol and caramelize the sugars in the meat.

4 Add the diced pork rind, carrot, olives, orange zest, cinnamon, and bay leaf. The pork rind will melt into the broth and thicken the juices during the long cooking. Pour in the red wine and enough water to completely submerge the meat, season with pepper (no salt yet) and bubble up.

5 Turn down the heat and cover the pot tightly. (Seal it with a flour and water paste if the fit is not perfect.) Allow to simmer very gently over a low heat or transfer to the oven, set at 325°F. Leave the daube to cook for 1½–2 hours, until the meat is so tender you can cut it with a spoon.

6 Remove the lid towards the end of the cooking to allow the juices to reduce and thicken. Taste and add salt before serving.

**SERVING SUGGESTION** ~ Serve with white rice or floury boiled potatoes dressed with chopped parsley. To follow, offer a winter salad of bitter leaves, such as dandelion, chicory, and endive.

# bœuf bourguignon

## SLOW-COOKED BEEF *in* RED WINE

This is a dish of lean beef enriched with fat pork, cooked in the same type of wine you intend to drink with the dish—and that should be a robust red burgundy with plenty of tannin, nothing too light or sharp. Older recipes include a calf's foot, which is precooked and added along with the pork skin. You can include a handful of button mushrooms if you wish—brown them in bacon fat at the same time as the onions.

Serves 6

**3½lb rump or silverside, cut into bite-sized cubes**
**a small bunch of parsley, thyme, and a bay leaf**
**1 bottle burgundy or any robust red wine**
**1 tablespoon brandy**
**1 heaped tablespoon all-purpose flour**
**½ teaspoon crushed allspice berries**
**salt and freshly milled pepper**
**8oz belly pork**
**1 tablespoon sweet butter**
**1½lb pickling onions, skinned**
**2 garlic cloves, crushed**
**1½ cups finely diced fatty bacon,**

৩০৯

1 Put the beef in a roomy bowl with the herbs, wine, and brandy. Leave to marinate overnight. Next day, remove the meat and shake it dry it over the bowl. Reserve the meat and the marinade.

2 Season the flour with allspice, salt, and pepper. Pat the beef dry and dust lightly with the flour, then set aside. Skin the pork, roll up the skin and tie it in a roll. Cut the meat into cubes.

3 Heat a heavy flameproof casserole and gently fry the pork cubes in their own rich fat until they brown on all sides and produce plenty of oily drippings. Remove the meat and reserve.

4 Reheat the pan drippings if necessary (you may need a little butter) and fry the beef until it browns, then remove and

reserve. Reheat the pan drippings, add the onions, garlic, and bacon and toss over the heat to brown everything a little.

5 Return the reserved meats to the pan, add the rolled-up pork skin and the marinade, bring to the boil and bubble up for 1–2 minutes until the liquor no longer smells of alcohol.

6 Turn down the heat, cover tightly and leave to simmer very gently for 2–3 hours. Alternatively, preheat the oven to 300°F and transfer the casserole to the oven. If you need to add liquid during cooking, make sure it is boiling.

7 When the meat is perfectly tender, remove the roll of pork skin, cut it into fine strips and stir it back into the juices. Remove the herbs. Taste and adjust the seasoning. Serve the beef from its cooking pot.

**SERVING SUGGESTION** ~ Serve with plain buttered white rice or pommes de terre mousseline (see page 94)—mashed potato beaten with plenty of hot cream, butter, and an egg yolk, and seasoned with nutmeg.

*The discovery of a new dish does more for the happiness of mankind than the discovery of a new star.*

**Anthelme Brillat-Savarin,** French gourmet (1755–1826)

# steak au poivre

## PEPPERED STEAK

This is a simple dish, requiring nothing less than perfection in the raw materials: the tenderest steak, lightly marbled with golden fat; the most aromatic pepper; the freshest butter; and good wine. Curnonsky, styled the Prince of Gastronomes as much for his appetite as by virtue of authorship of the Larousse Gastronomique, gives two recipes for his favorite dish, one including shallots, the other omitting them. I have chosen the latter, as the man himself said, "Faites simple." Serve with crisp fat frites—chips—with a salad to follow.

Serves 4

**4 steaks, about 12oz each**
**4 teaspoons cracked black peppercorns (use a mortar**
**and pestle to crack the pepper)**
**1 teaspoon salt**
**about ½ stick sweet butter**
**2 glasses white wine (half a glass per steak)**

TO FINISH
**chilled butter**

∽∾

1 Heat the serving plates. Coat each steak thoroughly in pepper, pressing the spice well in on both sides. Season each steak lightly with salt.

2 In a heavy pan, melt a nugget of butter per steak. When very hot, put in the steaks. Sear the meat on both sides, then continue cooking very slowly until they are cooked to your liking. Allow 2 minutes a side for very rare or up to 5 minutes for steak that is well done.

3 Remove the meat and transfer to the warm plates. Deglaze the pan by splashing in the wine and bubbling it up while scraping in all the little brown bits. Bubble to reduce by half. Whisk in an extra knob of butter to add gloss and thicken the sauce. Pour the sauce over the steaks.

# entrecôte vigneronne

## VINTNER'S STEAK

This rich Lyonnais version of the classic wine-sauced steak of the French bistro menu is deliciously simple. Choose well-hung steak with a generous lip of golden fat.

∽

Serves 4

4 thick-cut entrecôte steaks, about 12oz each
salt and coarsely milled pepper
6 tablespoons butter, chilled
2–3 shallots, finely chopped
1 onion, finely chopped
2–3 canned anchovy fillets, drained and finely chopped
½ cup robust red wine, preferably Burgundy

1 Trim the steaks neatly, leaving plenty of creamy yellow fat and season them on both sides. Melt 4 tablespoons of the butter in a heavy skillet.

2 Place the steaks in the pan as soon as the butter begins to foam. Sear the meat on both sides, then turn down the heat a little and cook for 3 minutes on each side if you like your meat rare or 4 minutes for medium. "Well done" steak is unthinkable. Remove and reserve in a warm place for the meat to settle and firm up while you make the sauce.

3 Add the shallots, onion, and anchovies to the juices in the pan, heat vigorously and cook for about 5 minutes, until the onions are lightly browned.

4 Stir in the wine, bring to boil, and bubble fiercely for 1–2 minutes to evaporate the alcohol and concentrate the flavors. Cut the remaining cold butter into tiny pieces and stir them into the sauce to add gloss and finish. Reheat until the butter melts and forms an emulsion, and transfer to a warm sauceboat. Serve the sauce with the steaks.

**SERVING SUGGESTION ~ Accompany the steaks with pommes allumettes—fine-cut chips—and hanks of watercress for the sake of the digestion.**

# entrecôte bordelaise

### RIB STEAKS *with* BEEF MARROW AND RED WINE

T his is one of the great dishes of the world. The only
essential is a butcher who knows his business. The meat
should be of a satisfying carmine, marbled, and edged with a
thick border of fat whose color varies from buttery gold to
creamy white—the color being dependent on breed, age, and
diet—and the marrow-bones of impeccable freshness.

∽

Serves 4

**4 thick-cut entrecôte steaks, about 12oz each
oil or melted butter for brushing**

SAUCE
**1 tablespoon sweet butter
2–3 shallots, finely chopped
4 tablespoons red wine (Bordeaux, naturally)
4 thick slices beef marrow
rough sea salt and freshly milled black pepper
freshly grated nutmeg
1 tablespoon chopped parsley**

TO SERVE
**a big bunch of watercress**

1 Have serving plates warming ready for the meat. Brush the steaks with oil or melted butter, and pepper them lightly on both sides.

2 Preheat a ridged griddle pan. (If you have a charcoal barbecue, so much the better—use that.) Grill the steaks until done to your liking: allow 2 minutes a side for very rare or up to 5 minutes for well done. Transfer the steaks to hot plates and reserve in a warm place while you finish the sauce.

3 Heat the butter in a small pan and gently fry the shallot until it softens—do not let it brown. Add the red wine and bubble fiercely for 3–4 minutes until the smell of alcohol has disappeared. Slip in the slices of beef marrow and remove from the heat.

4 Spoon the marrow and sauce gently over the steaks—each should have its slice of marrow. Season with grainy sea salt, freshly milled pepper, a little nutmeg, and a speckle of parsley. Serve the steaks immediately, with a generous hank of watercress on each plate.

**PREPARING BEEF MARROW** ~ Beef marrow or bone marrow, is found in marrow bones. Ask your butcher to saw a beef shin bone in short lengths. Take the package home, crack the bones with a hammer and lift out the soft yellow marrow inside. Poach the marrow for 1–2 minutes in simmering salted water—do not let the water boil. Lift the marrow out with care (it is fragile stuff), allow to cool, and slice it into thick medallions. You will probably have more than you need for the recipe—no matter— dice the rest and freeze it. You can use it to enrich sauces as if it were butter.

# hachis parmentier

## MEAT AND POTATO GRATIN

This sophisticated cottage pie was named for Monsieur Parmentier, the man responsible for persuading the French to plant potatoes.

❧

### Serves 4

½ stick butter
1lb ground lamb or leftover
cooked lamb, finely chopped
1 garlic clove, chopped
1 large onion, finely chopped
1½ cups chopped mushrooms,
½ teaspoon dried thyme
1 tablespoon chopped parsley
1 heaped tablespoon all-purpose flour
½ teaspoon ground allspice
1–2 bay leaves
1 cup stock or a mixture of white wine and water
salt and freshly milled pepper

### TOPPING
2½lb potatoes boiled and mashed with butter, milk, salt,
pepper, and a little nutmeg
1 egg yolk, forked up
1 tablespoon grated cheese
1 large nugget sweet butter

1 Melt the butter in a heavy pan and fry the meat, garlic, and onion until the meat changes color. If using cooked lamb, add it after the onion and garlic have cooked a little and just let it feel the heat. Stir from time to time to prevent sticking. Remove and reserve.

2 Reheat the pan drippings, add the mushrooms, salt lightly, sprinkle with thyme and parsley, and fry until they yield their juices, dry and begin to sizzle and brown. Remove and reserve.

3 Return the meat and onion mixture to the pan, sprinkle in the flour and fry for a moment. Season with allspice and pepper, add the bay leaves and stock or water and wine, and bubble up. Turn down the heat and leave to simmer for 20–30 minutes, until the meat is tender.

4 Meanwhile, preheat the oven to 400°F. Taste the meat and adjust the seasoning. The mixture may need a little more water—it should be juicy rather than dry.

5 Butter a gratin dish and spread a layer of mashed potato (about a third) in the base. Cover with the meat, then with half the remaining potato. Spread with the reserved mushrooms. Cover with a final topping of potato.

6 Fork up the potato and glaze it with egg yolk. Sprinkle with grated cheese and dot with butter. Finish in the oven for 20–30 minutes to reheat the layers and brown and crisp the top.

# navarin d'agneau

SLOW-COOKED LAMB *with* BABY VEGETABLES

Tender lamb and young vegetables, in season at the same time, are combined in this classic stew from the bourgeois tradition. Ask the butcher for some lamb bones for a stock.

❧

Serves 4–6

2 tablespoons oil or melted sweet butter
2½lb boneless lamb, such as neck fillet, shoulder
or breast, trimmed and diced
1 tablespoon diced lean Bayonne ham or bacon
20 small shallots or baby onions
1–2 carrots, diced
salt and freshly milled pepper
1 tablespoon all-purpose flour
2 garlic cloves
1 tablespoon tomato paste
a small bunch of parsley, thyme, and a bay leaf
4 cups lamb or vegetable stock

TO FINISH
new potatoes, fresh peas, young beans,
baby carrots, baby turnips
2 tablespoons chopped parsley

1 Heat the oil or butter in a straight-sided sauté pan or heavy skillet. Add the lamb, ham or bacon, shallots or onions, and carrots. Fry over a very brisk heat, stirring to brown the ingredients on all sides. Season with salt and pepper.

2 Spoon out any visible fat from the pan, sprinkle with the flour and toss over the heat for a couple of minutes to allow the flour to brown a little.

3 Add the garlic, tomato paste, herbs, and stock. Bring to the boil, bubble up for a minute or two, turn down the heat and simmer for 40–60 minutes, until the lamb is perfectly tender and the juices are concentrated and rich. Alternatively transfer the ingredients to an ovenproof casserole and cook in the oven for 1 hour at 325°F.

4 For a classic presentation, cook the baby vegetables separately in a ladleful of the stock from the lamb. Taste the lamb and adjust the seasoning. Pile the lamb in a warm serving dish and sprinkle with chopped parsley. Arrange the vegetables over the navarin before serving.

# épaule d'agneau en pistache

## POT-ROAST LAMB *with* LOTS OF GARLIC

For this recipe, a boned-out shoulder of lamb (it could be a leg or a saddle) is cooked with an unreasonable amount of garlic, the diagnostic ingredient of a pistache. Choose the mild rosy-skinned garlic of Provence and be brave—the quantity may seem like a lot, but the long, slow cooking melts the flesh, thickens the juices and gentles the flavor. Partridge, pheasant, and pigeons all benefit from the same treatment. Potatoes sautéed with rosemary are the perfect accompaniment.

Serves 4–6

1 shoulder of lamb, boned, rolled and tied
salt and freshly milled pepper
2 tablespoons fresh pork lard or goose fat
1 thick slice, about 4oz unsmoked raw ham or lean unsmoked
bacon, cut into small cubes
50 garlic cloves, about 5 whole heads, skinned but left whole
½ cup white wine (not too dry—a sweetish wine
complements the garlic)
⅔ cup lamb or vegetable stock
a small bunch of thyme, rosemary, bay leaf, and parsley
a small piece of dried orange peel

1 Preheat the oven to 350°F. Wipe the meat and rub it with very little salt and plenty of pepper.

2 Heat a roomy casserole which will just accommodate the meat and garlic. Melt the lard or goose fat in the casserole, add the ham and the garlic, and fry them until the garlic softens. Remove and reserve.

3 Turn the lamb in the hot drippings to brown it a little on all sides. Add the reserved ham and garlic, wine, and stock—the liquid should come about half way up the meat. Tuck in the herbs and orange peel and bring to the boil. Cover tightly and transfer to the oven.

4 Leave to cook for 1 hour, until the meat is perfectly tender and the garlic cloves melted and soft. Transfer the lamb to a warm serving dish, tent with foil, shiny side in, and leave to rest for 10 minutes before slicing into neat rounds.

5 Meanwhile, remove the herbs from the cooking liquor. Mash the garlic into the cooking juices to give the sauce body and fragrance, and spoon it over the meat.

# blanquette de veau

POACHED VEAL *in* CREAM SAUCE

A delicate dish that needs little preparation but requires a great deal of patience: it is very soothing both to make and to eat. Blanquette de veau is good for invalids, children, and toothless old granddads.

❧

Serves 6–8

4½lb boneless veal shoulder, trimmed and cut into cubes
8 cups veal or chicken stock, plus a little extra
1 small onion stuck with 2–3 cloves
2 carrots, diced
1 leek, finely chopped
a small bunch of parsley, thyme, and a bay leaf
½ teaspoon white peppercorns
6 tablespoons sweet butter
⅔ cup all-purpose flour
3 heaped cups button mushrooms
juice of 1 lemon
3 egg yolks
⅔ cup heavy cream
¼ teaspoon freshly grated nutmeg
sea salt and freshly milled pepper

TO FINISH
finely chopped parsley

1 Put the veal in a roomy cooking pot with the main quantity of stock. Bring to the boil and skim carefully, removing all the gray foam that rises.

2 Add the onion, carrots, leek, herbs, peppercorns, and salt. Bring back to the boil, turn down the heat and cover loosely. Leave to simmer gently (no bubbles should break the surface) for about 1½ hours, until the veal is perfectly tender and the broth strong and clear. Skim the broth every now and again, and add boiling water, if necessary, to maintain the volume of liquid in the pot.

3 Remove and discard the herbs, onion, and carrots with a draining spoon and discard. Remove and reserve the meat. Strain the broth carefully, pouring it through a sieve lined with a clean cloth. Return the broth to the pot—you need the full 8 cups.

4 Turn your attention to the sauce. Mash the butter with the flour until it makes a smooth paste—this is a beurre manié. Whisk the paste into the broth and reheat, whisking throughout, until boiling. Reduce the heat and simmer for 30 minutes or so, until the sauce has reduced by a third of its volume and is smooth and shiny.

5 Meanwhile, bring a little veal or chicken stock to the boil. Add the mushrooms and 1 teaspoon of the lemon juice and cook for 5 minutes. Add the reserved meat and reheat gently, then transfer to a warmed serving dish.

6 Fork the remaining lemon juice with the egg yolks. Remove the sauce from the heat and whisk in the cream, then the egg

yolk mixture. Season with a little nutmeg. Return the pan to the heat and simmer for a few minutes, stirring with a wooden spoon, until all is smooth. Do not let the sauce boil. Taste and season with salt and pepper.

7 Pour the sauce over the meat and shower with parsley.

# *choucroute*

## SAUERKRAUT *with* SAUSAGES

This stupendous pork-and-cabbage one-pot dish is prepared in Alsace and where the German influence is strong. It takes its name from the diagnostic ingredient, choucroute or sauerkraut, salt-barreled cabbage.

∾

Serves 8

4lb sauerkraut
4 thin slices fresh pork fat
1 large carrot, sliced
1 onion stuck with 2–3 cloves
a small bunch of parsley, thyme, and a bay leaf
1 teaspoon juniper berries, crushed
1 pork knuckle
1lb smoked pork loin or bacon in one piece
8 thick slices ham
1 large garlic sausage, about 2lb, pricked
8 tablespoons goose fat or freshly prepared pork lard
2 glasses white wine
about 4 cups stock or water
8 large frankfurters
salt and pepper

TO SERVE
boiled potatoes/pickled cucumbers/mild mustard

1 Put the sauerkraut in a bowl of cold water and work it with your fingers to loosen the strands. Drain off the water. Repeat twice, squeezing to remove as much of the liquid as possible. Spread the drained sauerkraut on a clean tea towel and leave to dry for 1–2 hours. Season with pepper—it should not need salt.

2 Preheat the oven to 325°F. Line a roomy flameproof and ovenproof braising pot or casserole with the pork fat. Spread half the sauerkraut on the fat, then add the carrot, onion, herbs, juniper berries, pork knuckle, smoked pork or bacon, ham, and garlic sausage in layers. Sprinkle with half the goose fat or lard and top with the remaining sauerkraut.

3 Pour in the white wine and enough stock or water to ensure that all the ingredients are moistened. Finish with the remaining goose fat. Bring the ingredients to the boil, cover tightly with a lid or foil and transfer to the oven.

4 Leave to cook gently for 2 hours, until almost all the liquid has been absorbed. After 30–40 minutes, remove the garlic sausage and keep it warm. After 1 hour, remove and reserve the bacon. After 1½ hours, remove and reserve the smoked pork.

5 To finish, 20 minutes before the end of cooking, heat the frankfurters in enough simmering water to cover—do not allow the water to boil.

6 Pile the sauerkraut on a heated serving dish—a long and narrow dish is traditional. Remove and discard the onion and separate the meats. Pile the meats, sliced as appropriate, on top of the sauerkraut: the traditional arrangement is a lower layer of sliced ham topped with alternating overlapping slices of bacon,

sausage, and pork. Finally, the frankfurters should be arranged around the edge.

7 Serve very hot, on hot plates, with a big bowl of plain cooked potatoes, pickled cucumbers, and mild mustard.

**CHOUCROUTE** ~ The choucroute is prepared with finely shredded white cabbage, which undergoes a process of light fermention. This miraculous transformation not only makes it taste good but preserves the vitamin content and makes it easier to digest. The brine is used as a cure for everything from hangovers and morning sickness to the aftermath of childbirth.

The new-season choucroute is traditionally eaten with fresh pork and sausage after the autumn pig-killing, which conveniently coincides with the wine harvest. It is then eaten with salt pork and smoked sausages throughout winter, and reappears with goose for the Christmas festivities. It takes a bow on New Year's Day, as an oblation for the year's renewal, and the last of the barrel is scraped in Lent, to be eaten with fresh fish as soon as the spring thaw releases the fishing boats from harbor.

SWEETBREADS (RIS) ~ To prepare, put the sweetbreads in a bowl and cover them with salted water. Leave for 24 hours to soak out any traces of blood. Clean and wipe. Then put them into boiling water with a few peppercorns and 1 tablespoon vinegar. Bring back to the boil and simmer for 15 minutes. Drain and remove all traces of skin and sinew. Press between two plates, placing a weight on top, until cold and firm. Cut into squares. They are now ready to be finished—stewed in butter; sauced with mushrooms and cream; egged-and-breadcrumbed and fried—the choice is yours.

BRAINS (CERVELLES) ~ Soak them first in salted water (2–4 hours depending on the size of the brain). Remove the covering membrane and wipe the meats carefully. Soak them for a further 1 hour to get rid of any remaining blood. Simmer as for sweetbreads—brains will need an extra 10 minutes' cooking. Store them in their cooking liquid if they are not be used at once.

TRIPE (TRIPES) ~ This is neither more nor less than the lining of the stomach of a ruminant, preferably a beef animal. But be warned, French butchers don't necessarily steam and bleach their tripe before they sell it to you, so it may be spongy and somewhat unappetizing until well-scrubbed and scalded. All ruminants, including the cow, have 4 stomachs —3 are labelled gras double, the fourth is just tripe. All four are used for France's most famous tripe-dish, tripes a la mode de Caen. To prepare the recipe for six, buy 4lb ready-scrubbed tripe and stew very gently—preferably in a round-bellied, narrow-mouthed tripière—with a couple of blanched, split pig's trotters, a handful of sliced carrots, a couple of thickly sliced onions, parsley, bay leaf, a splash of calvados, peppercorns, salt, and enough cider to cover. When the tripe is perfectly tender—3–4 hours at a very gentle simmer—serve with boiled potatoes and eat with a spoon.

LIVER (FOIE) ~ Calves' liver is, quite rightly, considered the most delicate of variety meats, and foie de veau à l'anglaise—calves' liver English-style —is the most appreciated. To prepare for four servings of à l'anglaise, have your butcher slice 1lb calves' liver in finger-length fillets, soak in milk for half an hour, drain, toss in a little seasoned flour and fry in butter over a high heat with a handful of diced bacon—the liver should still be pink and juicy.

KIDNEYS (ROGNONS) ~ Veal kidneys are the most prized of the group: to prepare kidneys à la bordelaise for two, slice a veal kidney thickly (nick out the fatty white core), soak in water with a splash of wine vinegar for 10 minutes, drain, toss in a little seasoned flour, fry in butter for a minute or two till the meat stiffens, add a splash of madeira and a glass of red Bordeaux, bubble up to evaporate the alcohol and thicken the sauce, and finish with a spoonful of mild Bordeaux mustard. Rognons blancs—white kidneys—the tactful way of describing testicles—can be prepared in the same way.

# ris de veau à la crème

## VEAL SWEETBREADS *with* CREAM

Two varieties of sweetbreads are sold under the same name: the pancreas (elongated in shape and found near the stomach) and the thymus glands (rounded and to be found at the base of the throat).

∽

Serves 4

**4 veal sweetbreads**
**a few black peppercorns**
**1 tablespoon white wine vinegar**

SAUCE
**2 tablespoons sweet butter**
**2 tablespoons finely chopped button mushrooms**
**1 tablespoon all-purpose flour**
**⅔ cup white wine**
**⅔ cup heavy cream**
**1 egg yolk, forked to blend**
**salt and freshly milled pepper**
**rounds of bread, fried in butter, to serve**

1 To prepare the sweetbreads, put them in a bowl and cover with cold water, then add a little salt. Set in a cool place for 24 hours to soak out any traces of blood. Clean and wipe.

2 Poach the drained sweetbreads for 3 minutes in boiling water with the peppercorns and vinegar. Drain and remove all traces of skin and sinew. Press between two weighted plates until cold and firm—at least 1 hour. Slice thickly.

3 Meanwhile make the sauce. Melt the butter in a small pan and fry the mushrooms gently for 2–3 minutes. Sprinkle with the flour, stir over the heat until the butter has been absorbed, then add the wine. Bubble up, whisking over the heat, until the sauce no longer smells of raw alcohol.

4 Stir in the cream and the egg yolk, reheat until just below boiling, then slip in the sweetbreads. Reheat gently, taste, and season with salt and pepper, and serve on little rounds of bread fried in butter.

# pieds de porc
## sainte-ménéhould

BREADED PIG'S TROTTERS

The chief pleasure of a trotter is texture—long, slow cooking makes the meat and skin soft and gelatinous. The secret is the long stewing in a wine-flavored court bouillon (cooking broth). If you start them first thing in the morning you can leave them to simmer all day.

❧

Serves 4–8

**4 pig's trotters, singed, scalded, and scraped**
**1 onion, cut into chunks**
**1 carrot, cut into chunks**
**1 celery stick, cut into chunks**
**1 bay leaf**
**a few peppercorns**
**1 glass dry white wine**

TO FINISH
**4 tablespoons fresh bread crumbs**
**1 garlic clove, finely chopped**
**2 tablespoons chopped parsley**
**generous 2¼ sticks sweet butter, melted**
**salt and freshly milled pepper**

1 Split the trotters in half lengthwise, tie the halves back together again in pairs and pack them in a flameproof casserole that can also be put in the oven. Add the onion, carrot, celery, bay leaf, and peppercorns. Add the wine and enough water to cover the ingredients completely.

2 Bring to the boil, cover loosely, and cook steadily for 30 minutes. Top up with boiling water, turn down the heat and cover tightly, sealing with a flour-and-water paste if the lid does not fit perfectly. Preheat the oven to 275°F.

3 Place in the oven and leave to simmer very gently for at least 8 hours, until the trotters are really soft. Leave them to cool in their liquid.

4 Drain the trotters and reserve a ladleful of the cooking liquid. Untie and arrange in a gratin dish, cut side up. Remove the hard central bones. Preheat the grill.

5 To finish, mix the bread crumbs, garlic, and parsley. Top the trotters with the breadcrumb mixture, season with salt and pepper and trickle with melted butter. Grill to gild and crisp the topping.

# cervelles au beurre noir

## BRAINS *with* BLACK BUTTER

A delicate dish. French gourmets have a more robust view of what is good to eat and they would not dream of discarding the best bits of any beast.

❧

### Serves 4

**1 calf's brain or 3 lambs' brains**
**½ teaspoon peppercorns**
**1 bay leaf**
**1 tablespoon vinegar**
**salt and freshly milled pepper**

TO FINISH
**generous 2¼ sticks sweet butter**
**a little all-purpose flour**
**1 tablespoon vinegar**
**1 tablespoon drained capers**

1 Soak the brains in salted water for 2–4 hours, depending on size. Drain, pat dry, remove the covering membrane and wipe carefully. Soak for another hour in fresh salted water to get rid of any remaining blood.

2 Bring a small pan of water seasoned with salt, the peppercorns, bay leaf, and vinegar to the boil and slip in the brains. Bring back to the boil, turn down the heat and simmer for 10–15 minutes, depending on size. Drain well and press between two plates until cold and firm.

3 Meanwhile, begin by clarifying the butter ready for finishing the dish: melt it in a small pan. As soon as it oils, pour the clear liquid off the top and reserve, discarding the milky liquid that has drifted to the bottom.

4 Slice the brains into bite-sized squares, dust thoroughly with a little seasoned flour, and fry in a tablespoon of the clarified butter until browned. Remove the brains and reserve.

5 Heat the remaining butter in the pan. As soon as it turns a nutty brown—do not let it burn—add the vinegar and the capers, reheat and spoon the butter over the brains.

sauces

# sauce béchamel

## BASIC WHITE SAUCE

Béchamel is one of three foundation sauces on which a wide range of others are based; sauce espagnole and sauce velouté are the other two foundation sauces. A béchamel rarely stands on its own but serves as a vehicle for other ingredients—cooked, finely diced, or chopped chicken, meat, fish, or vegetables (particularly spinach). These can then be transformed into plats composées, combined dishes—they can be spread in a gratin dish, finished with a topping of grated cheese or bread crumbs and butter, and browned under the broiler until it bubbles and gilds.

Makes 2½ cups coating sauce

**½ stick sweet butter**
**½ cup all-purpose flour**
**2½ cups full-cream milk**
**salt and freshly milled pepper**
**¼ teaspoon freshly grated nutmeg (optional)**

1 Melt the butter in a heavy-based pan. Stir in the flour and let it fry for a moment until it looks sandy—do not let it take color. This is a white roux.

2 Allow the pan to cool while you heat the milk in another pan. Remove the milk from the heat just before it boils.

3 Whisk the boiling milk slowly into the roux, return the pan to a gentle heat and stir with a wooden spoon until the sauce is smooth, no longer tastes of raw flour, and is thick enough to coat the back of the spoon.

4 Taste and season with salt, pepper, and a pinch of grated nutmeg (if using). To keep the sauce for later, drop a few pieces of cold butter over the surface to melt and prevent a skin from forming.

**SAUCES DERIVED FROM SAUCE BÉCHAMEL** ~ For a richer sauce, use light cream instead of milk.

*Sauce mornay* ~ Add 3–4 tablespoons grated cheese and reheat gently until the cheese melts.
• For seafood gratins, fold cooked seafood (fillets of sole, turbot or salmon; peeled prawns; dressed crab; scallops; or mussels) into sauce mornay and spread in a gratin dish. Finish with more grated cheese or bread crumbs and slip under the broiler to brown.
• For individual fish gratins, use well-scrubbed scallop shells as the containers.
• The milk can be replaced with the same volume of white wine and fish stock and finished with an extra knob of butter or 1 tablespoon cream.

*Sauce soubise* ~ This is an onion sauce based on béchamel. Cook 14oz finely chopped onion in ½ stick butter until tender (do not let the onion brown). Puree with a spoonful of cream. Stir the puree into the béchamel, reheat, taste, and season.
• A soubise is traditionally served as a sauce for hard-cooked eggs or plain boiled potatoes.

*Sauce duxelles* ~ Make a basic béchamel with white wine, chicken stock and cream instead of milk. Gently cook 4 cups chopped mushrooms (wild or cultivated) in about ½ stick sweet butter—keep going until the juices have all evaporated but do not let the fungi brown. Stir the cooked mushrooms into the sauce.

- Good for filling vols-au-vent or choux buns.
- Perfect as a coating sauce for the meat from a boiled chicken —spread in a gratin dish, coat with the sauce, sprinkle with fresh bread crumbs, dot with butter and gild under the broiler.

*Sauce panada* ~ This is a thick white sauce base which serves as a vehicle for other ingredients. Halve or quarter the volume of liquid to fat and flour, depending on the density of the sauce required for the recipe. Experience will tell you what you need.
- A panada can be diluted with other liquids—broth or wine— to make a pouring sauce, or used as the basis for a savoury soufflé—suitably flavored with grated cheese, diced ham, finely chopped shrimp or chopped cooked spinach.
- As the basis for croquettes, make a panada following the béchamel recipe, but with 1 cup milk or stock. Combine with chopped leftover cooked chicken or meat; cooked mushrooms; or grated cheese. Leave to cool and firm up overnight in the fridge. Then form it into little cork shapes, dust in seasoned flour, dip in forked-up egg and coat with a jacket of bread crumbs. Allow the coating to set for 1–2 hours before deep-frying the croquettes. The temperature of the oil should be sufficiently high to crisp the coating while allowing the interior to heat—if it is too hot, the jacket will burn; too cool and it will burst. Practice makes perfect.

# sauce espagnole

## BASIC BROWN SAUCE

One of the three most important sauces of the French kitchen (the others are the white béchamel and the velouté), this dark, rich meat-based sauce takes its identity and character from the salt-cured wind-dried ham of Bayonne. Bayonne ham is closely identified with the serrano hams which color and flavor every Spanish stew—hence the name Spanish sauce. The French refinement is the inclusion of jambon de Bayonne in the mirepoix, a flavoring-mix that adds depth and complexity to the finished sauce. While sauce espagnole needs no further attention as an enhancement for meat-based dishes, it also provides the foundation for other sauces.

Makes about 2½ cups

**2 tablespoons sweet butter**
**1 tablespoon finely diced Bayonne ham**
**1 large carrot, diced**
**1 onion or 2 shallots, finely chopped**
**1 celery stick, finely chopped**
**2 tablespoons chopped mushrooms**
**1 bay leaf**
**1 small thyme sprig**
**¼ cup all-purpose flour**
**4 cups strong meat stock, heated**
**2½ cups chopped tomatoes**
**salt and freshly milled pepper**

1 Melt half the butter in a heavy, preferably copper-based, pan. Add the ham, carrot, onion or shallots, celery, mushrooms, bay leaf, and thyme, and fry very gently for 20–30 minutes until soft and lightly caramelized. Remove and reserve—this is a basic mirepoix, the classic flavoring-fry of the French kitchen.

2 Melt the rest of the butter in the pan, sprinkle in the flour and stir over the heat until the mixture turns a deep brown color—mahogany is too dark—and remove immediately. Add a splash of stock to halt the cooking process.

3 Return the mixture to the heat and bubble up, whisking until you have a smooth sauce base—a caramel-colored panada. Whisk in the remaining stock and bring back to the boil.

4 Add the reserved mirepoix and the tomatoes and bubble up again, beating to amalgamate everything thoroughly. Turn down the heat and leave to simmer very gently—no bubbles should break the surface—for 2–3 hours, until the sauce has reduced by half and it is well flavored and a little sticky. Skim the sauce every now and then during cooking.

5 Allow to cool a little, then pass the sauce through a fine sieve or, even better, strain it through a muslin cloth. To prevent a skin from forming, drop a few scraps of butter over the surface to melt. Use as the foundation for other sauces to accompany plain-broiled or spit-roasted meats.

### SAUCES DERIVED FROM SAUCE ESPAGNOLE ～

*Sauce Robert* ～ To 2½ cups sauce espagnole, add ⅔ cup white wine and 4 tablespoons white wine vinegar. Bubble up until reduced by a third. Remove from the heat and stir in 1 tablespoon Dijon mustard.
• Use to sauce broiled pork chops, pan-broiled magrets de canard (duck breasts—start cooking them skin side down and leave them pink), spit-roast rabbit, or poached eggs.

*Sauce bordelaise* ～ To 2½ cups sauce espagnole, add 1 cup light red wine (a Bordeaux, for authenticity) and bubble up until the sauce is reduced in volume by a third. Poach 4oz beef marrow in salted water for 10 minutes. Drain carefully, cut off and reserve 4–6 slices, and dice the rest. Reheat the sauce gently and then stir in 1 tablespoon sweet butter, cut into small pieces, the cubed marrow and, finally, 1 tablespoon finely chopped parsley.

• Use to sauce broiled entrecôte steaks, topping each steak with one of the reserved marrow slices.
• Use the sauce as a binding agent for diced cooked beef or lamb for a gratin. Spread in a gratin dish, top with bread crumbs and finely chopped parsley and dot with butter. Slip the gratin under the broiler to crisp and bubble.

*Sauce madère* ~ To 2½ cups sauce espagnole, add ⅔ cup Madeira, then bubble up until reduced by a quarter.
• Use to sauce hot ham slices or pan-grilled pork escalopes.
• Use as the binding agent for diced cooked meat—lamb, pork or beef—when making a gratin, as for sauce bordelaise.

*Sauce périgourdine* ~ To 2½ cups sauce Madeire stir in 1 tablespoon diced black truffle and reheat gently. For extra richness, melt in a spoonful of mashed pâté de foie gras or confit de foie gras (see page 28).
• Use to sauce broiled magret de canard (duck breast), breast of chicken or guinea fowl.
• Use as the binding agent for cooked poultry or game when making a gratin as for sauce bordelaise.

*Sauce au poivre* ~ To 2½ cups sauce espagnole, stir in 1 teaspoon well-crushed peppercorns (do this in a mortar). Bring to the boil and simmer for 10–15 minutes, until the sauce is thoroughly impregnated with the pepper. Stir in 2–3 tablespoons heavy cream, bubble up again and use to sauce broiled steaks.

# sauce velouté

## VELOUTÉ SAUCE

The third member of the roux-based group of French sauces—the other two are espagnole and béchamel. This smooth golden sauce is made by simmering a well-reduced flour-thickened chicken or veal stock (or a fish fumet, if you intend the sauce for a fish dish). For a paler result, instead of cooking a roux, thicken the sauce with a beurre manié—flour worked to a paste with its own volume of cold butter. This sauce can be used as the basis for a chicken, vegetable, or fish gratin.

Makes about 4 cups

**6 tablespoons sweet butter or goose fat**
**⅔ cup all-purpose flour**
**6¼ cups strong chicken or veal stock**
**small knob of butter to finish (optional)**

1 In a roomy, heavy-based pan, melt the butter or goose fat. Sprinkle in the flour and stir until it looks sandy.

2 Whisking to keep it smooth, pour in the stock, and bring to the boil. Allow the sauce to give one big belch, turn down the heat and simmer gently, stirring regularly, for 30 minutes or so, until the sauce has lost a third of its volume and is smooth and shiny. If preparing the sauce in advance, float a few scraps of butter over the surface to prevent a skin from forming.

## SAUCES DERIVED FROM THE VELOUTÉ ~

*Sauce allemande* ~ Prepare a chicken velouté and cook it for an extra 30 minutes. Prepare the same volume of stock as sauce, flavoring it with mushroom peelings, strain it and add to the sauce. Simmer gently for another 30 minutes until the sauce forms a thick coating on the back of a wooden spoon. Remove from the heat and allow to cool a little. Fork 2 egg yolks with 1 tablespoon heavy cream and whisk into the sauce. Reheat the sauce gently, whisking until well-blended, and remove from the heat before it boils. Season with a little freshly grated nutmeg.
• Use to sauce sautéed liver or kidneys; poached, sliced sweetbreads or brains; or poached eggs. To sauce fish, apply the same method using a fish velouté.

*Sauce poulette* ~ Finish a sauce allemande (as above) with the juice of 1 lemon and 2 tablespoons finely chopped parsley.
• Serve with poached chicken or use as a sauce for vineyard snails (see page 30).

*Sauce suprême* ~ Finish a sauce allemande by adding
2–3 tablespoons heavy cream and a squeeze of lemon juice.
• Use to sauce poached or plain-roast barnyard birds—chicken,
guinea fowl or duck.

*Sauce aux câpres* ~ To a chicken or fish velouté, add
1 tablespoon well-drained pickled capers.
• Use to sauce boiled beef from pot-au-feu (see page 200) or
serve with poached fish, such as turbot, cod or salmon.

*Sauce Nantua* ~ Prepare a fish velouté and simmer to reduce
by half. Add an equal volume each of single cream and fish
stock made with crustacean debris—heads and shells of
crayfish, shrimp and/or lobster. Bubble up, reduce the heat and
leave to simmer gently for 30–40 minutes, until reduced by a
third. Season the sauce with a little cayenne pepper and whisk
in a few nuggets of chilled, sweet butter.
• Serve with poached fillets of sole or as a sauce for lobster,
prawns or scallops.

# *beurre blanc*

## MELTED BUTTER SAUCE

This simple emulsion of melted butter and wine vinegar is delicate and delicious. Make more than you think you need—people can never get enough of it.

Serves 4

**2 shallots or 1 small onion, finely chopped**
**5 tablespoons white wine vinegar**
**2¼ sticks sweet butter, chilled and chopped into small pieces**

1 Cook the shallots or onion with the vinegar in a small pan. When the vinegar has reduced by half, to about 4 tablespoons, strain it and discard the shallots or onion.

2 Return the vinegar to the pan. Whisk in the butter, gradually adding it in small pieces, with the pan over a very low heat or by the side of the heat so that the butter melts into a thick sauce. Do not let the sauce boil. If, in spite of your best efforts, the mixture splits, let the sauce cool and start again adding a tablespoon of boiling water.

# sauce hollandaise

## HOLLANDAISE SAUCE

This hot butter sauce thickened with egg yolks is made in much the same way as a béarnaise, though the flavoring is lemon juice rather than a reduction of vinegar and shallot. This is a delicate sauce well suited to the white-fleshed fish, such as sole, turbot, plaice, cod, haddock, or scallops, that are caught in the cold waters of the North Atlantic. It also goes well with soft-coddled or poached eggs and is perfect with spring vegetables, particularly new potatoes, cauliflower, and asparagus.

Makes about 2½ cups

**2 cups sweet butter**
**4 egg yolks**
**1½ tablespoons lemon juice**
**salt**

❧

1 First clarify the butter: melt it gently in a small pan until runny. Continue heating gently until the fat and the whey separate, allowing the water to sink to the bottom. You can now pour the liquid butter from the surface leaving the whey behind, or allow the mixture to cool and lift off the solids, discarding the liquid beneath.

2 Put 4 tablespoons boiling water and the clarified butter in a fairly small pan of either enamel or copper lined with tin but not aluminum (which reacts with the acidity in the lemon, turning the sauce green). Place the pan into a second pan half filled with cold water. Alternatively, use a double-boiler.

3 Place the pans over a moderate heat. Fork the egg yolks with 2 tablespoons cold water and whisk them into the butter. Stir with a wooden spoon until the mixture thickens to the consistency of a pouring custard. When the water in the outer pan boils, the sauce will be thickened enough.

4 Remove from the heat and add the lemon juice slowly—if you add it too fast, the sauce will split and you will have to emulsify it again with a quick blitz in a blender. Taste the sauce and add salt.

# *sauce béarnaise*

## BÉARNAISE SAUCE

T his sauce of butter and egg yolk is flavored with a robust reduction of wine vinegar, shallot, and tarragon and served with broiled meat. It is a speciality of Béarn, birthplace of Henri 1V, royal gourmet and a man much admired for his desire to put a chicken in every Frenchman's pot. The cooking of Béarn is rich and luxurious, making plentiful use of goose fat in everyday cooking, saving the butter for best. Serve with broiled meat (steaks, lamb chops, veal cutlets, pork escalopes), or broiled fish (swordfish, tuna, mackerel—nothing too delicate).

☙

Makes about 1 cup

4 tablespoons wine vinegar
1 shallot, finely chopped
2–3 tarragon and chervil sprigs
4 large egg yolks
2¼ sticks sweet butter, chilled and diced
1 tablespoon tarragon leaves
salt and white pepper

1 Put the vinegar, shallot, tarragon, and chervil in a small enamel pan, bring to the boil and bubble fiercely until the volume is reduced by half. Remove the pan from the heat, strain, and allow the liquid to cool a little.

2 Meanwhile, whisk the egg yolks with 2 tablespoons cold water in a bowl. Whisk in the vinegar reduction. Place the bowl over a pan of simmering water. Whisk the sauce over a gentle heat until the mixture thickens like a custard.

3 Add the cold butter piece by piece, whisking throughout, until you have a thick-ish, spoonable sauce. If the mixture looks like curdling—separating or scrambling—remove the pan from the heat and place the base in cold water, then whisk in a little cold water and carry on whisking until the sauce regains its smoothness. Stir in the chopped herbs (if using).

4 To keep the sauce warm until you are ready to serve it, set the pan back over the bain-marie—do not allow the water to boil. If it curdles when cold, whisk in a tablespoon of hot water.

### SAUCES DERIVED FROM BÉARNAISE ~

*Sauce valois* ~ Combine the basic béarnaise recipe with a little meat glaze—a strong reduction of a beef-bone broth (see page 74). Use to sauce roast game—venison or wild boar.

*Sauce choron* ~ Combine the basic béarnaise with 1 tablespoon warmed tomato puree and season with a little lemon juice. Use to sauce broiled fish, poached or soft-cooked eggs, broiled tournedos (fillet of beef), or sautéed noisettes of lamb.

# beurre maître d'hôtel

## PARSLEY BUTTER

A useful little preparation to have to hand in the back of fridge, this flavored butter—literally, head-waiter's butter —is designed to melt on contact with hot food, providing an instant sauce for plain-broiled fish, steaks, chops, lamb cutlets, or steamed vegetables. French butters, traditionally unsalted, are naturally pale rather than golden—a result of the particular breed of cow, the pastures on which the herds graze, and an absence of additives. The flavor, too, is distinctive, since the cream, the raw material of the butter, is allowed to ripen a little, giving the finished product a distinctive, slightly soured flavor and helping to preserve it in the absence of salt. The butters of Normandy, particularly those traded in the town of Isigny, are the most prized, not least because they melt to a creamy smoothness.

Serves 8 (sauces 8 portions)

**2¼ sticks unsalted French butter, softened**
**juice of 1 lemon**
**2 tablespoons finely chopped flat-leaf parsley**
**½ teaspoon salt**

1 Beat the softened butter until light and creamy. Beat in the lemon juice little by little. Beat in the parsley and season with a little salt. All this can be done in the food processor.

2 Sandwich the soft butter between 2 sheets of plastic wrap and pat it out to the thickness of a pencil. Leave to cool and harden in the fridge for 1 hour, then either cut it into a dozen little squares with a knife, or cut into the same number of little disks with a scalloped pastry cutter.

3 Store in the fridge for a week or in the freezer for as long as you wish (well, a month or two). In a warm kitchen it will defrost sufficiently in 10 minutes. The food to be sauced should be hot enough to melt the edges of the butter on contact and it should not be dropped into place until just before you serve. Watching the butter melt is part of the pleasure.

## OTHER USEFUL BUTTERS ~

*Beurre à l'ail (garlic butter)* ~ For garlic bread this is prepared by pounding 4 fresh garlic cloves with 1 teaspoon salt and blending the resulting mush thoroughly with 1 cup softened sweet butter. A milder garlic butter (preferred in the north of France and served as an accompaniment to cold hors d'œuvre) can be made by blanching and softening the garlic cloves in salted water first—10 minutes at a fast simmer.

*Beurre d'anchois (anchovy butter)* ~ This is a piquant alternative to a maitre-d'hotel butter—just pop a pat on broiled meats or plain-cooked fish to melt in the heat. The preparation also appears on the hors d'œuvre table—good with a bunch of rosy radishes settled on a bed of cracked ice. To prepare, pound 6–8 anchovy fillets (from a can, drained of their oil) with 1 cup softened sweet butter.

*Beurre de crevettes (prawn butter)* ~ This is made by preparing a strong reduction of a broth made with the debris of peeled prawns (shells, heads) with flavoring herbs—parsley stalks, bay leaf, leek tops, and peppercorns. Use 2 tablespoons of the reduction to flavor 1 cup softened sweet butter. You can include the prawn meat if serving the butter as part of a seafood hors d'œuvre or with cold poached salmon or turbot. The same process will produce beurre de crabe or d'homard—crab or lobster butter. Shellfish butters are also used to enrich, lightly thicken and give a shine to seafood sauces: cut the chilled butter into small pieces and whisk it piece by piece into cooking broth. Miraculously, the hot broth and the cold butter form an emulsion. Serve without delay—it won't hold for long.

# coulis de tomate

## FRESH TOMATO SAUCE

*A coulis is a runny puree, a preparation of raw vegetables or fruit, which can be used as a sauce as it is or can be added to other sauces as an anhancement.*

Serves 4

**2lb field-ripened tomatoes
juice of 1 lemon
sugar to taste
salt and freshly milled pepper**

1 Pour boiling water over the tomatoes in a bowl to loosen the skins, then peel. Slice the tomatoes in half through the equator. Scoop out the jelly and pips and push through a sieve, discarding the solids and reserving the juice.

2 Put the tomato flesh and juice in the blender or food processor with the lemon juice. Reduce all to a smooth puree. Season with pepper, a little salt, and a pinch of sugar, more if necessary. Serve as a sauce for grilled fish. Or, alternatively, stir it into mayonnaise to make a dressing for prawns or fish.

# *vinaigrette*

## OIL AND VINEGAR DRESSING

The vinaigrette is used to dress a salade verte, a green salad, which is served after a main course. The inclusion of non-leaf ingredients turns it into a salade composée, a mixed salad, whose proper place is among the hors d'œuvres. Some like to eat it as a mop for the last of the meat-juices, others prefer to eat it with the cheese course or as a palate refresher for dessert.

❦

Makes enough to dress a salad for 4

**1 tablespoon wine vinegar**
**½ teaspoon salt**
**3 tablespoons olive oil**

1 Mix the vinegar and salt first, working with a fork to dissolve the crystals before adding the oil, a medium in which the salt crystals cannot dissolve.

2 Add the oil, blend thoroughly, and toss with the salad leaves, well rinsed and patted dry, just before serving. Finish with a dusting of freshly milled black pepper if you wish—though this is not necessary if the oil has a sufficient degree of pepperiness.

**SAUCE RÉMOULADE** ~ To convert the vinaigrette to a sauce rémoulade, start with 1 tablespoon mild mustard—Dijon or Pommery—and work in the vinegar and oil. This is the classic dressing for celery root salad but is excellent on a green salad, beet or potato salad.

**FRENCH SALADS** ~ An astonishing variety of edible leaves, both cultivated and wild, are available in French markets throughout the year. All are eaten as salads when young and tender, though the same leaves may appear later in the year as cooked vegetables. When designed for a salad, the choice is for texture and flavor—bitter or mild, crisp or soft, sweet or sharp—with a view to complementing the dishes the salad is designed to precede or follow.

If the main course is, say, a robust meat dish, a touch of bitterness is appropriate—frisée (curly-leafed chicory), endive, dandelion (pis-en-lit—a diuretic, as its name implies). If the main course is fish, the leaves chosen should be equally delicate: lamb's lettuce (mâche), young spinach. If the main course is rich and creamy—butter-roast chicken, a creamy fish dish, a quiche or a gratin dauphinois—the choice will be for mustardy leaves such as arugula, watercress or the refreshing sharpness of sorrel.

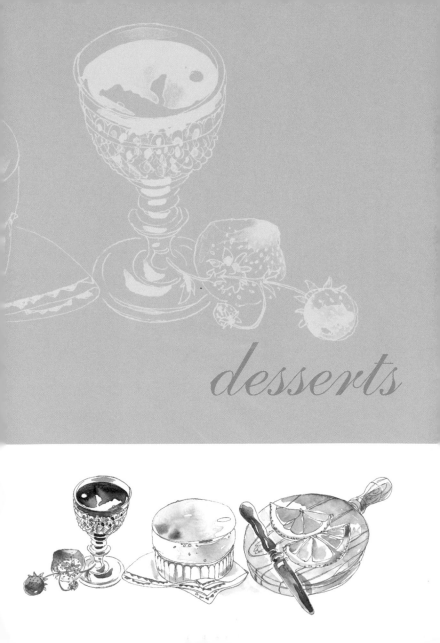

_desserts_

# sirop

## STOCK SYRUP

A basic stock syrup, sterile and storable in the larder, can be used to sweeten anything you please without the bother of dissolving sugar crystals. Use to sweeten fruit salads, fruit coulis, and berry vinegars. As a soaking syrup for babas, flavor with rum (see page 318).

Makes about 2 cups

**2 cups water**
**2 cups superfine sugar**

1 Pour the water into a small pan. Add the sugar and dissolve it in the water over a gentle heat.

2 Bring to the boil and simmer for 10 minutes, until reduced by a third. Remove from the heat and leave to cool. Bottle in sterilized jars and seal tightly for storage—no need to keep it in the fridge.

# praline

## CARAMELIZED NUTS

*The praline is a flavoring ingredient in its own right, used in much the same way as chocolate, vanilla, or coffee and kept conveniently to hand in the storecupboard.*

Makes about 2 cups

**2 cups blanched almonds**
**1½ cups superfine sugar**

1 Line a baking sheet with non-stick baking parchment. Roast the almonds gently in a dry pan until lightly toasted all over, stirring to avoid burning—remove as soon as they change color.

2 Melt the sugar with 1 tablespoon water in a copper pan, stirring until the crystals have completely dissolved. Bubble up and cook until the syrup turns pale brown—4–5 minutes.

3 Add the almonds, stir for 1 minute, and remove from the heat. Pour on to the prepared baking sheet and leave to cool.

4 Pound the praline in a mortar and store in it a stoppered glass jar until required.

# *coulis de framboise*

## RASPBERRY COULIS

A simple fruit puree sweetened with sugar syrup, this is one of the basic sauces of the French dessert table. It can be used as a foundation for creamy desserts as well as to sauce anything and everything which might benefit from its sharpness and intensity of flavor. Other berries suitable for a coulis are blueberries, black currants, and strawberries (for these, add a little lemon juice to bring out the flavor).

Makes 2½ cups

**1lb fresh raspberries**
**1½ cups superfine sugar**
**1 tablespoon lemon juice**

1 Pick over the raspberries, discarding hulls and any mouldy berries. Transfer to a food processor or blender. Add the sugar and lemon juice, and blitz until you have a smooth puree. Sieve to remove the pips.

## USING COULIS DE FRAMBOISE ~

- As a sauce for creamy desserts—ice cream, bavarois, cream-stuffed pastries.

- As a flavoring for the dessert itself. For flavoring a hot soufflé, fold with egg yolk and proceed as for Grand Marnier Soufflé (see page 280). For a mousse, dissolve a little sponged or soaked gelatin in the coulis and fold in whipped cream and firmly whisked egg white. For an ice cream, stir raspberry coulis into its own volume of crème anglaise (see page 266) lightened with whipped cream, freeze until almost solid, beat to a foam with an egg white, and freeze again until firm.

**NOTE** ~ Foods served frozen need more vigorous flavoring than foods to be eaten at room temperature. Sweeten the puree more than you think necessary, and sharpen it up with a squeeze of lemon.

# crème pâtissière

## CONFECTIONER'S CUSTARD

This is a rich egg custard thickened with cornstarch for a smooth finish—older recipes use wheat flour.

❧

Makes about 3 cups

2½ cups full-cream milk
short length of vanilla pod
3 egg yolks
scant ½ cup superfine sugar
½ cup cornstarch
2 tablespoons sweet butter

1 Add the vanilla pod to the milk and bring to the boil in a heavy-based pan. Remove from the heat, lift out the vanilla, and scrape the seeds into the milk, then discard the pod.

2 In a roomy bowl, whisk the egg yolks until fluffy. Whisk in the sugar, a tablespoonful at a time, and continue whisking until the mixture is white and light. Sprinkle in the cornstarch and whisk until combined.

3 Gradually add the hot milk, whisking until all is blended. Pour the custard back into the pan and bring to the boil, whisking throughout, and boil for 1 minute until smooth and thick. Tip the custard back into the bowl, dot with butter to prevent a skin from forming, and leave to cool.

4 Use to fill pastries, such as choux buns, éclairs, or pancakes; spread in a tart base and top with fresh fruit.

## PREPARATIONS DERIVED FROM CRÈME PÂTISSIÈRE ~

*Crème au beurre (French butter cream)* ~ This is a confectioner's custard made firm enough to set into a layer without support—useful for layering up a sponge-cake, assembling a mille-feuille. Cut 1 cup softened sweet butter into small pieces and gradually whisk them into the hot crème pâtissière. The custard will thicken as it cools and the butter solidifies.

*Crème au chocolat (chocolate cream)* ~ Melt 4 squares dark plain chocolate with the milk when you bring it to the boil with the vanilla, and proceed as above.

*Crème au café (coffee cream)* ~ Stir a little very strong, very black coffee into the milk.

*Crème praliné (praline cream)* ~ Stir in 3–4 tablespoons well-pounded praline (see page 261) when the cream has cooled.

*Crème anglaise (pouring custard)* ~ Dilute the main recipe with its own volume of light cream plus a little milk, if you like it even runnier.

*Île flottante (floating island)* ~ Make a crème anglaise (above) with 6 egg yolks, reserving 4 of the whites. Whisk the reserved whites with 4 tablespoons superfine sugar to make a meringue and use 2 tablespoons to form egg-shaped meringues. Poach the meringues gently in simmering water for a few minutes until set. Float these soft meringues, the "islands," on the custard.

# sabayon

## WHISKED WINE CUSTARD

A pouring sauce which takes the place of a crème anglaise when serving pastry-based desserts—fruit tarts or feuilletés.

Makes 6 cups

**6 fresh free-range eggs**
**6 tablespoons superfine sugar**
**about ¾ cup white wine**

1 Crack the eggs into a bowl which will fit over a pan. Whisk the eggs until fluffy. Add the sugar gradually and whisk until white and light—about 5 minutes with an electric beater (that is, twice as long as you think). Whisk in the wine.

2 Place the bowl over a panful of water—the water should simmer rather than boil—or use a bain-marie where the base of the bowl should be clear of the water. Whisk the mixture until it is firm enough to hold the mark of the whisk.

3 Remove from the heat and cool the bottom of the basin in cold water to halt the cooking process. Use to sauce desserts or as the basis for an ice cream flavored with a fruit liqueur—Cointreau, Grand Marnier, Crème de Cassis.

# glace à la vanille

## VANILLA ICE CREAM

Nothing is simpler or more delicious than a plain vanilla ice cream—a revelation. Perfect with meringues, as a filling for choux buns, with fresh berries and a crisp langue de chat. For a lighter ice, omit the cream. For a glace au chocolat (chocolate ice cream) melt 4 squares dark chocolate into the milk before you remove it from the stove. For a glace au café (coffee ice cream) flavor the milk with instant coffee diluted with a little boiling water, or mix in a tiny cup of strong coffee. For a glace praliné (praline ice cream) fold in 2 tablespoons praline (see page 261) after you fold in the whipped cream. For a glace aux fruits (fruit ice cream) replace the whipped cream with 1¼ cups fresh fruit puree—strawberry, raspberry, blueberry, peach, apricot or banana—or combine the finished mixture with an equal volume of prepared fruit coulis (see page 262).

Makes about 4 cups

**1½ cups full-cream milk**
**½ vanilla pod**
**4 egg yolks**
**4 tablespoons superfine sugar**
**1 cups heavy cream**

1 Bring the milk and vanilla pod to the boil in a roomy pan, remove from the heat, cover and leave to infuse for 30 minutes in a warm place. Scrape the little sticky seeds from the pod and add them to the milk, discarding the pod.

2 Meanwhile whisk the egg yolks and sugar in a bowl until light and pale. Whisk in the infused milk. Set the bowl over a pan of simmering water and keep the water at a gentle bubble. Stir the custard constantly until it is thick enough to coat the back of a wooden spoon. Remove from the heat, transfer to bowl and leave to cool completely.

3 Lightly whip the cream and fold it into the custard. Transfer to a container for freezing. When the ice cream is half-frozen, remove from the freezer and beat the mixture thoroughly to break up the ice crystals. Freeze it again until firm.

4 Transfer the ice cream from the freezer to the fridge 30 minutes before serving to let it soften a little.

# sorbet aux fraises

## STRAWBERRY WATER ICE

The sorbet, as its name suggests, takes its cue from the chilled syrup-flavored waters much appreciated in Arab lands. At its simplest, a sorbet is nothing more than frozen flavored water beaten to increase the volume and lighten the texture. The inclusion of either egg white or a dash of some form of distilled liquor—fruit brandy, Calvados, marc—produces a softer consistency since neither substance actually freezes solid. To prepare a sorbet cassis (black currant sorbet), poach 1lb black currants in 1¼ cups stock syrup (see page 260) until the fruit collapses—4–5 minutes. Allow to cool, sieve or liquidize in a blender. To prepare a sorbet framboise (raspberry sorbet), stir 1lb raspberries and 1 tablespoon lemon juice into scant 2 cups boiling stock syrup. Allow to cool and push through a sieve or liquidize in a blender. To prepare a sorbet au citron (lemon sorbet), add ⅔ cup lemon juice to 2½ cups stock syrup—taste, add more sugar if the flavor is too bland, or add water if it's too sharp.

Makes about 3 cups

**1lb ripe strawberries, hulled**
**juice of 1 lemon**
**1 cup stock syrup (see page 260)**
**1 egg white**

1 Pick over the berries, chop roughly, then mix with the lemon juice and the stock syrup. Push through a sieve or tip everything into a blender and process to a puree.

2 Freeze the puree in an ice cream maker or transfer it to a metal or plastic container and place in the freezer until just crystallized. Beat thoroughly to break up the ice crystals. Taste and add more lemon juice or extra sugar if the flavor is too subtle—freezing masks sweetness.

3 Whisk the egg white, then whisk it into the sorbet. Beat thoroughly to increase the volume and lighten the texture. Freeze until firm.

# petits pots à la crème

## VANILLA CREAM CUSTARDS

*A simple dessert, this is exquisite with the little fraises de bois that come into the markets in early spring—the smaller the berry, the more intense the flavor. They are also heaven with wild strawberries, sliced peaches, or orange segments dressed with a splash of Cointreau. To prepare crèmes caramel (caramel custards), drop a little caramelized sugar into each ramekin before you pour in the custard. To prepare a caramel, heat 3 tablespoons superfine sugar with a little water until the sugar crystals melt, bubble up until the sugar browns. Then swirl a little of the caramel around the base of each ramekin. The caramel will melt and spread of its own accord, making a sticky little brown sauce.*

∽

Serves 6

**2 eggs and 4 egg yolks**
**2½ cups single cream**
**3 tablespoons superfine sugar**
**seeds scraped from a short length of vanilla pod**

1 Preheat the oven to 325°F. Prepare a roasting pan with six little ramekins in it.

2 Whisk the whole eggs and the yolks with the cream and sugar—or whiz them up in a food processor. As you whisk or whiz, add the tiny seeds scraped from the vanilla pod.

3 Divide the custard among the ramekins—each should be about half full. Pour enough boiling water into the roasting pan to come half way up the outsides of the ramekins. Cover the baking tray with foil, shiny side down.

4 Bake for 45–50 minutes, without allowing the water to boil again, until the custards are set round the sides but still soft in the centre.

5 Remove the ramekins from the water and leave to cool. Refrigerate for an hour or two—longer if necessary.

# *petits pots au chocolat*

## LITTLE CHOCOLATE POTS

O ne of the few desserts the French cook prepares at home, this is the simplest but most delicious of all chocolate desserts. Neither a mousse nor a custard but something in between, the secret of success lies in the quality of the chocolate and the freshness of the eggs (save the whites to make meringues —see page 290). Perfect with almond tuiles or any crisp little biscuit. The usual strictures about raw eggs apply.

Serves 4–6

**5 squares best-quality dark chocolate
(at least 70% cocoa solids)
4 tablespoons orange juice, heated to just below boiling
4 eggs, separated
1 teaspoon finely grated orange zest
about 1 tablespoon superfine sugar**

1   Break the chocolate in small pieces and place in a bowl set over simmering water. Add the orange juice and stir until melted and perfectly smooth.

2   Remove the bowl from the heat and beat in the egg yolks one by one—they will cook and thicken a little in the residual warmth. Allow to cool to finger temperature.

3   Whisk the egg whites until perfectly stiff. Fold the egg whites into the chocolate with the orange zest, and taste to make sure the mixture is sweet enough: if not, fold in a little superfine sugar.

4   Spoon into individual soufflé dishes or, if you have them, special purpose-made chocolate pots. Set them in the fridge for a few hours to firm

**MELTING THE CHOCOLATE** ~ If the heat is too high, the chocolate will change texture and look grainy—the chocolatière's word is "seize," an exact description of what happens. To return the chocolate to its liquid state, beat in a little warm clarified butter or oil and beat it until it is smooth.

**VARIATIONS** ~ The basic chocolate mixture can be varied as follows:
• For petits pots au café, replace the orange juice with the same volume of strong black coffee.
• For petits pots à la cannelle, melt the chocolate with coffee, as above, and stir in a pinch of powdered cinnamon.

# crème brûlée

## BURNT CREAM

In the days when every rural household in dairy country kept a milk-cow, the first spring milkings which became available after the birth of her calf, were as thick and rich as butter. When ladled into a shallow dish, this exceptionally creamy milk set quite solidly enough to be given a caramel topping without the need to thicken it first with egg yolk. Hence the name— burnt cream. This is a creamy custard topped with caramelized sugar—simple but delicious. Before we all had the benefit of eye-level broilers, the sugar topping was melted with a salamander—a red-hot iron heated on the stove.

Serves 4

**1 cup heavy cream**
**short length of vanilla pod**
**1 tablespoon sugar**
**3 egg yolks**

1 Preheat the oven to 325°F. Warm the cream to blood temperature with the vanilla pod. Stir in the sugar to dissolve it. Whisk in the yolks. Take off the froth, remove the vanilla pod, and pour the custard into 4 individual ramekins. Set them in a roasting pan. Pour enough boiling water into the roasting pan to come half way up the outside of the ramekins.

2 Bake for 30–40 minutes, until the custards are set but not hard—they should have just a little give, but not wobble all over the place. Check them during the cooking to make sure they do not scramble. Let the custards cool in the fridge for 8 hours—where they will set a bit more.

3 When you are ready to serve, preheat the broiler. Sprinkle the surface of the custards with a thin, even layer of brown sugar. Dip your hand in cold water and sprinkle a few drops on the sugar—only enough to dampen it slightly. Pop the ramekins under the very hot broiler to caramelize the sugar. If you have a blow-torch in the tool kit, that's a very good way of doing it. Classically delicious.

# bavarois aux framboises

RASPBERRY MOUSSE

*I*n *the midst of gloom induced by contemplating modern life,
philosopher-novelist Michel Houellebecq allowed the hero of
Atomised to find solace in sweet things: "He ordered a
raspberry bavarois and two glasses of kirsch: it was time to
return to simple pleasures."*

Serves 6–8

**1 oz leaf gelatin, about 12 leaves, or 2 sachets powdered gelatin**
**generous 2 cups superfine sugar**
**juice of 1 lemon**
**3 cups fresh or frozen raspberries**
**2 cups heavy cream**
**sweet almond oil or any flavorless oil for brushing mold**

1 Both leaf and powdered gelatin need soaking in cold water
before they are added to a recipe. If using leaf gelatin,
cover with cold water and leave until soft—5 minutes or so—
then squeeze dry. If using powdered gelatin, sprinkle it over
4 tablespoons cold water and leave for 5 minutes without stirring,
until it goes spongy. The gelatin is now ready for use and can be
stirred into a hot liquid without worrying that it will make the

mixture lumpy. If you are adding gelatin to a cold liquid, melt the soaked or sponged gelatin gently first, without stirring, in a bowl over hot water.

2 Dissolve 1⅛ cups of the sugar in ⅔ cup boiling water, stirring until the crystals have dissolved. Warm to just below boiling, then remove from the heat, add the lemon juice and the gelatin and stir until well blended. Allow to cool a little.

3 Save a few of the most perfect raspberries for decorating, then combining the rest with the gelatin mixture. Transfer to a blender and process to a puree, then sieve.

4 Tip the mixture into a bowl and leave it to cool to a soft set— 2–3 hours in the fridge. Choose a single large jelly mold, or pick 12 individual molds (small tumblers make a pretty shape), and brush with almond oil—cold water will do, but the unmolded bavarois may not be quite so perfect.

5 Whip the cream with the remaining sugar. Fold into the softly set jelly, turning it over gently with a metal spoon until well blended. Spoon the mixture into the prepared mold(s) and transfer to the fridge for another 2 hours, until set.

6 To unmold, rinse a serving plate with cold water (this will allow you to slide the dessert gently into place if necessary). Run hot water over the outside of the mold, and place the plate on top. Turn the plate and the mold over together and shake to loosen. Remove the mold and finish with the reserved raspberries.

# soufflé au grand marnier

## SOUFFLÉ *with* ORANGE LIQUEUR

My maternal grandmother, a belle from Baltimore and a friend of Wallis Simpson, employed a real French pastry chef whose speciality this was. I was sixteen before I was allowed to taste it, which was a little unfair since I had been allowed to wield the whisk on the eggs since I was ten. The flavoring can be Cointreau or Curaçao or any other sticky liqueur that takes your fancy. Good with a langue de chat (see page 324), almond tuile, or any other crisp little biscuit.

### Serves 4

**6 eggs plus 3 egg whites**
**1¼ cups superfine sugar**
**4 tablespoons Grand Marnier**
**finely grated zest and juice of 1 orange**
**½ teaspoon salt**
**butter and superfine sugar for the soufflé mold**
**confectioner's sugar for dusting**

1 Preheat the oven to 400°F. Have ready a soufflé mold, 8–9 in in diameter, well buttered and sprinkled with superfine sugar.

2 Separate the eggs, reserving the yolks and adding the whites to the extra 3 whites and reserve. Whisk the yolks in a bowl, adding the sugar spoonful by spoonful, and carry on whisking until the mixture is fluffy and pale.

3 Fold in the Grand Marnier, 2 tablespoons of the orange juice and 1 teaspoon of the zest. Whisk the egg whites with the salt until they hold their shape. Using a metal spoon, fold them into the whisked yolks, turning the mixture gently to blend the ingredients thoroughly.

4 Spoon the mixture into the soufflé mold—it should be about two-thirds full—and run a knife between the mold and mixture to encourage an even rise. Transfer to the oven and bake for 20 minutes.

5 Open the oven very carefully and check that the top is well risen and crusty—if it is still a little trembly, return it for another 5 minutes (don't bang the oven door as you close it). Dust with confectioner's sugar and serve immediately.

**NOTE** ~ While the soufflé is baking, make a little orange sauce by simmering 1¼ cups freshly squeezed orange juice and the zest cut into fine matchstick strips with enough sugar— 4 tablespoons—to make a sticky syrup. Finish with a knob of butter chopped into little pieces and a tablespoon or two of whatever liqueur you have used to flavor the soufflé.

# crêpes sucrées

## SWEET CRÊPES

*S* *weet crêpes are rarely eaten on their own but serve as*
*containers for jams or flavored custards, with which they*
*are stuffed and rolled, or folded in four like a pocket-hankie.*

Serves 4 (about 12 pancakes)

**1 cup all-purpose flour**
**1 tablespoon vanilla sugar**
**2 eggs**
**1¼ cups milk**
**1 tablespoon brandy or Calvados**
**butter for greasing the pan**

1 Sift the flour into a bowl and mix in the sugar. Make a well in the middle and work in the egg and enough milk to give you a batter with the consistency of light cream. Leave it to develop for an hour or two. Stir in the brandy or Calvados.

2 Heat a small skillet. Roll a small knob of butter around it. When it foams, pour in enough crêpe batter to coat the base of the pan. If you tip in too much, pour the excess back into the bowl immediately.

3 Let the batter set over the heat—when the top surface is dry, flick the crêpe over to brown the other side. Flip it out on to a clean cloth. Tuck it up to keep it warm. The first crêpe never works properly. Treat it as a test run to tell you if the pan is hot enough and to get the right amount of mixture. Continue until all the batter is used up.

## DISHES DERIVED FROM CRÊPES SUCRÉES ~

*Crêpes Normande* ~ Fill the crêpe with apple puree flavored with Calvados, roll up or fold in four to enclose the filling. Arrange in a gratin dish, sprinkle with sugar and heat in the oven until piping hot and lightly caramelized on top. Serve with the thick slightly soured cream of Normandy.

*Crêpes cévenoles* ~ Fill the crêpe with chestnut puree, sweetened, and flavored with rum. Finish as for crêpes Normande.

*Crêpes à la confiture* ~ Spread the crêpe with jam and roll up like bolsters. Finish as for crêpes Normande.

# galettes bretonnes

## BRITTANY PANCAKES

*The daily bread of the Bretons, a Celtic people with a
preference for griddle-cooking, is pancakes made with
buckwheat, a grain with a rough texture and a nutty taste
which lacks the glutin necessary for making bread and grows
under poor conditions where wheat cannot thrive. Although a
galette can be made with buckwheat alone, a proportion of
wheat flour lightens the mix.*

### Makes a dozen

**2 cups bread flour**
**2 cups buckwheat flour**
**1 level teaspoon salt**
**1 level teaspoon baking powder**
**2 eggs, forked to blend**
**1¼ cups milk**
**goose fat, oil or butter for greasing**

### TO SERVE
**12 tablespoons plum jelly**
**about 1 stick sweet butter**

1 Sieve the flours with the baking powder and salt and then whisk in the rest of the ingredients till you have a smooth cream. Leave for 10 minutes.

2 Heat a griddle or heavy skillet, grease it lightly with a cloth dipped in goose fat, oil, or butter, and test the heat with a drop of the mixture—it should sizzle and set immediately.

3 Pour on enough of the mixture to cover the base of the pan. Cook over a medium heat until the top looks dry. Flip it over and set the other side. Continue till all the mixture is used up. Keep the pancakes warm in a clean cloth while you work.

4 Don't roll the galettes, fold them into quarters and fill with plum jam and a knob of butter. Or roll and shred into noodle-like strips and serve with cream and honey.

**NOTE ~** For a savory version, use as a wrapper for a grilled sausage or a slice of bacon or enclose a raw egg in its folds.

# clafoutis aux cerises

## CHERRY BATTER PUDDING

A batter which is raised with eggs and nothing else sometimes it bounces up and sometimes it doesn't. No matter—it will be delicious anyway. Any small fruit that can be cooked in its skin will do—damsons, blueberries, blackberries, black currants—but if you choose black cherries, the juice bleeds beautifully into the golden crust. Wonderful with the thick yellow cream of Normandy. De-stalk, wash, and dry the cherries. Don't pit them— live dangerously.

❦

### Serves 4

**3 heaped tablespoons all-purpose flour**
**3 level tablespoons superfine sugar, plus extra for dusting**
**3 eggs, lightly whisked**
**scant 2 cups milk, warmed**
**¼ teaspoon vanilla seeds, scraped from the pod,**
**or a drop of vanilla essence**
**8oz black cherries**
**a big knob of butter**

### TO FINISH
**kirsch or dark rum—Negrita gives the right flavor (optional)**

1 Preheat the oven to 425°F. Fold the flour and sugar into the whisked eggs. Beat in the warm milk with the vanilla to make a smooth batter.

2 Preheat a baking dish—wide, shallow, and about the size of a small roasting pan—and drop in a small knob of butter. Roll the butter around the pan to grease it.

3 Tip in the batter—it will be sloppy—and sprinkle the cherries over. Dot with butter and bake for 25 minutes, until puffy and well risen.

4 Finish with a good sprinkle of the liquor (if using) and a thick dusting of sugar, and serve without delay, before it subsides.

# *beignets de pommes*

## APPLE FRITTERS

*T*he apples considered suitable for cooking are yellow
fleshed, sweet, and fragrant and are expected to hold
*their shape in the heat. The choice is usually between pommes
reinettes and Golden Delicious—les golden. In apple territory,
where beer or cider replace wine as the everyday refreshment,
the fritter batter is lightened with beer and flavored with
Calvados or some other white brandy—kirsch, eau de vie de
poire, or prune—which has the virtue of evaporating as soon as
it hits the skillet, leaving the coating crisp, airy and with a
subtle, flowery fragrance.*

Serves 4

**4 yellow-fleshed apples
1 tablespoon Calvados or kirsch plus a little extra
a little lemon juice
1 egg
1 cup all-purpose flour
1¼ cups light beer
oil for deep frying (lard is traditional)
sugar to sprinkle**

1 Peel and core the apples, slice them into rings about ⅛in thick, and reserve (you may if you wish sprinkle the slices with a little Calvados or kirsch). A sprinkling of lemon juice will prevent them from browning.

2 Break the egg into a bowl and whisk to combine the yolk with the white. Sift in the flour. Whisk vigorously to blend, adding the beer gradually until you have a thick cream that coats the back of a wooden spoon. Whisk in the Calvados or kirsch.

3 Heat a deep pan of oil for deep frying—do not stint, you need plenty. When a light blue haze rises from the surface— the sign that the oil has reached the right temperature— immediately dip a few slices of apple into the batter and drop them into the fryer. Add three or four at a time—no more, or the temperature will drop and the beignets will be soggy. A frying time of 3 minutes is enough.

4 Lift out the fritters, drain, and transfer to paper towels to soak up excess oil, then sprinkle with sugar. Continue until all are the fritters are done.

# *meringues chantilly*

MERINGUES *with* WHIPPED CREAM

A simple recipe which needs nothing more than patience both in the beating and the baking. The secret is the gentleness of the oven, a matter of drying out rather than baking: in high summer, it's possible to cook meringues in the heat of the sun alone. Save the yolks for a custard (see page 264) or to make mayonnaise (see page 163).

∞

Makes 12–14 meringues

**4 large egg whites**
**generous 1 cup superfine sugar**

TO FINISH
**whipped cream**

1 Line a baking sheet with non–stick baking parchment. Preheat the oven to 225°F or on the coolest setting. Leave the door ajar to keep the temperature as low as 167°F if possible. If the oven is too hot, the meringue will weep a sticky residue and it won't set.

2 Everything must be squeaky clean before you begin—the bowl, the whisk, the spoon with which you fold in the sugar. Above all, the egg whites must have no trace of yolk. Whisk the egg whites until light and white.

3 With a metal spoon, fold in half the sugar. Carry on whisking until firm and shiny. Fold in the remaining sugar and whisk until satiny and perfectly firm—the mixture should stay in the bowl if you turn it upside down.

4 Using 2 tablespoons, drop spoonfuls of meringue on to the prepared baking sheet. Bake for 3 hours, until perfectly crisp and dry. The middle should still be a little sticky. Cool and then sandwich the meringues together with whipped cream.

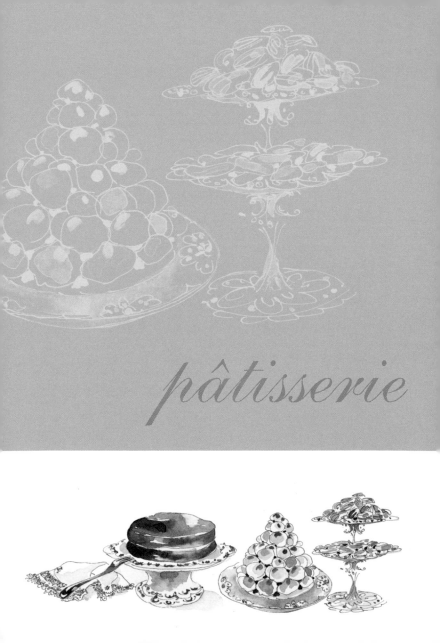

*pâtisserie*

# *pâte feuilletée*

PUFF PASTRY

Makes about 1lb

**scant 2¼ sticks sweet butter, chilled**
**2¼ cups all-purpose flour**
**½ teaspoon salt**

∽

1 Make the pastry in a very cool place. See that the butter is firm without being hard. Sift the flour with the salt into a roomy bowl. Cut in a third of the butter with a sharp knife until you have a mixture resembling fine bread crumbs.

2 Mix in about 2 tablespoons water—enough to make a dough that is soft but does not stick to the fingers. Knead lightly. Set the dough aside for 20 minutes, with the rest of the butter beside it so that pastry and butter both reach the same temperature.

3 Roll out the pastry to a thickness of about ⁄in. Dot with small pieces of butter the size of hazelnuts, using about a third of the total quantity. Then fold the pastry into three, like a napkin. Fold again into three, with the folds in the opposite direction. Set aside for 20 minutes.

4 Repeat the process twice more, rolling out the pastry, adding the same amount of butter each time and folding it. Set the pastry aside for 20 minutes after each process. Then leave it for

another 20 minutes before you roll it out and cut it into any shape you please.

5 Bake puff pastry in a hot oven 430°F for 20–30 minutes, until well risen, crisp, and golden.

**VOL-AU-VENT CASES** ~ For vol-au-vent cases choose two round cutters, one larger than the other. Using the larger of the cutters, cut the dough into neat rounds; with the smaller cutter, press a circle into the middle of each round without cutting through to the base. When the vols-au-vent are baked, the smaller disks can be lifted off to leave a hollow for the filling and making a lid to place on top. Vol-au-vent cases may be filled with a savory filling, precooked and bound with a creamy sauce.

**MILLE-FEUILLE** ~ For a sumptuous mille-feuille, roll out the pastry and cut it into three matching rectangles or circles, dust with confectioner's sugar and bake as usual. Allow to cool. Spread one pastry layer with crème pâtissière, top with another pastry layer and spread with strawberry jam and whipped cream. Top with the third layer and finish with a thick dusting of confectioner's sugar. The filling can, of course, be varied as you please.

**GALETTE** ~ For a galette, roll two circles of pastry and sandwich together with a layer of home-made marzipan—to prepare, make a paste with ground almonds, a little sugar and enough egg yolk to bind. Dampen the edges and press them together to prevent the marzipan from running out and prick the top to let the steam out. Plain the top with a little milk and egg, then bake as usual until puffed and crisp.

# *pâte sucrée*

## SWEET SHORTCRUST PASTRY

Makes about 1lb

1½ cups all-purpose flour
½ teaspoon salt
½ cup confectioner's sugar
1 stick very cold butter
2 egg yolks

1 Sift the flour into a bowl with the salt and sugar. Make a well in the middle and grate in the cold butter. Mix the ingredients lightly with a knife.

2 Fork the egg yolks with 1 tablespoon water, drop into the middle of the flour mixture and use your fingertips or the knife to gather all into a soft ball—if you need a little more water, sprinkle in the minimum.

3 Using the tips of your fingers (never the palms), knead the dough lightly for a few minutes, just long enough to form a soft ball—do not overwork it or it will oil and toughen. Wrap the dough in plastic wrap or cover with a clean cloth and leave in a cool place for 30 minutes.

4 Roll out the pastry on a floured board with a floured rolling pin—use short firm strokes, pressing rather than stretching—and cut into the required shape.

**PLAIN BISCUITS** ~ To make plain biscuits, cut out neat rounds with a wine glass or cookie cutter, prick with a fork to stop bubbling, transfer to a baking sheet and bake for 10–12 minutes at 200°C. Cool on the baking sheet for a few minutes to firm up slightly, then transfer to a wire rack to cool completely. The basic quantity makes 24 little biscuits.

# pâte à choux

CHOUX PASTRY

Makes about 1lb 10oz

**generous 1 stick butter**
**1¼ cups all-purpose flour**
**4 large eggs**

✦

1 Roughly chop the butter and put it in a heavy pan with
1¼ cups water. Bring to the boil and remove from the heat
as soon as the butter has melted.

2 Sift in the flour gradually, beating with a wooden spoon until
smooth—eliminate the visible pockets of flour. Set the pan
back on the heat and beat the mixture for a few minutes until it is
solid enough to leave the sides clean.

3 Remove from the heat, and allow the paste to cool to finger
heat. Beat in the eggs one by one, beating thoroughly
between each addition. At first the paste will seem reluctant to
accept the eggs; as you persist, it becomes easier to work, rather
as a mayonnaise becomes more malleable. At the end, the paste
should be shiny and fairly soft though still firm enough to hold its
shape when dropped from a spoon.

**CLASSIC CHOUX PASTRIES** ~ The classic choux pastry recipes are profiteroles (cream-filled choux buns), pets-de-nons (choux pastry fritters dusted with sugar) and the Burgundian gougère, a ring of choux pastry flavored and studded with cheese.

*Choux buns* ~ To prepare choux buns ready for stuffing, lightly butter a couple of baking sheets (not necessary if using non-stick sheets) and preheat the oven to 350°F. Scoop up nuggets of dough using 2 teaspoons and drop them on to the trays, allowing plenty of space between the dollops for the paste to expand.

Bake the buns for 35–40 minutes, until well puffed, brown, and firm. As soon as you take them out of the oven, slip a knife into their sides to let out the steam—if you do not do this, the pastry is likely to soften and collapse. If the insides are still a little doughy, scoop out excess dough with the handle of a teaspoon or round-bladed knife.

Transfer to a wire rack to cool, then stuff with sweetened whipped cream (crème Chantilly), crème pâtissière (see page 264) or home-made vanilla ice cream (see page 268).

*Croquembouche* ~ The French wedding cake is a tall pyramid of choux buns stuffed with crème pâtissière stuck together with caramelized melted sugar, a creation attributed to the great 19th century chef-pâtissièr, Marie-Antoine Caréme. When the moment comes for the cake to be shared among the guests, distribution is easy since all the bride has to do is hit the pile with a silver hammer, sending choux buns in all directions.

**PASTRY-MAKING TIPS ~**

• The cooler you can keep the pastry while you work, the lighter, crisper, and crumblier it will be when it comes out of the oven. This is easier to achieve if all your implements—mixing bowls, rolling pin, board—are made of chilly materials. Professional pastry chefs prefer china for the bowl, marble for the board and a tube of unbreakable glass filled with iced water as the rolling pin, though none of these are essential. If at any stage the pastry becomes too warm, it will begin to look oily and acquire a shine, a sign that the shortening has melted and the pastry will be heavy (carry on—it will still taste good even if it is a little tough).

• Shortening is any type of fat—lard, butter, margarine, goose fat—used in combination with flour to make pastry with or without additional liquid in the form of water or egg yolk and/or brandy. If using butter as the shortening, a useful tip is to pop it in the freezer until it hardens, then grate it into the flour for the preliminary mixing. The amount of extra liquid required depends on the amount of water naturally present in the shortening—some butters and "spreadable" margarines contain an amazing amount of water.

• Egg yolk acts as a binder for a rich pastry—one with a high proportion of shortening (which can make it overly crumbly when baked). If water is used, make sure it is iced—coolness really does make a difference. The replacement of plain water with alcohol—brandy—delivers a light, crumbly pastry since the alcohol evaporates when heat is applied.

• Proportions for a classic English pie-crust are 2:1 flour to shortening; for a very rich French pâte brisée, the proportions can go as high as 1:1, though this is very crumbly indeed unless you include sugar or grated cheese, both of which act as binders after cooking.

• When mixing a pastry, use the tips of your fingers (never your palm, which is far to warm) to work the shortening and the flour together, and lift them up in the air as you mix to incorporate as much air as possible.

• A resting period in a cool place—after the mixing and before the rolling—allows the flour to absorb the liquid and the fat to become firm, ready for rolling.

• When rolling out a pastry, pat it flat with the rolling pin before you start, then use short sharp strokes, pushing away from your body, pressing rather than stretching.

• When lifting and fitting the pastry into a tart pan, fold it over the rolling pin to support it along its length and ease it gently in place without stretching. If it is stretched, the pastry will shrink during the cooking.

• Allow plenty of edge to remain when trimming. When mending any holes (necessary to contain a runny filling) dampen the edges of the hole before patching gently with a little pastry.

• Do not overfill a pastry case, even if the recipe has landed you with too much filling, and make sure the filling does not come right up to the rim.

# tourte aux noix

## WALNUT TART

This is a nut tart from the Périgord, where walnuts are traditionally used to fatten the foie-gras goose. You can also make it with unskinned hazelnuts or almonds—a little roughness is essential for the texture.

❧

Serves 6

1¾ sticks butter
2 cups all-purpose flour
2 tablespoons superfine sugar
1 egg, forked to blend

### FILLING
1 egg white
1¼ cups heavy cream
1 cup walnuts, chopped or ground
(not too thoroughly, or the nuts will oil)
½ cup granulated sugar

### TO FINISH
6 tablespoons confectioner's sugar
1 tablespoon brandy
8–10 walnut halves

1 Make the pastry first. Using the tips of your fingers, rub the butter into the flour and sugar, and work in enough egg to give a light, firm dough. Cover with plastic wrap and set aside for 30 minutes.

2 Preheat the oven to 350°F. Roll out the dough on a lightly floured board with sharp strokes of the rolling pin and use it to line a 8in tart pan, preferably one with a removable base. Ease the pastry gently into the pan without stretching it. Trim leaving a generous rim of pastry—you don't want to lose any of the height.

3 Prick the base and bake the tart case (no need to fuss with beans and foil lining) for 10 minutes, until the surface looks white and dry.

4 Meanwhile, prepare the filling: whisk the egg white until stiff. Half-whip the cream. Mix the cream and egg white with the walnuts and sugar.

5 Remove the tart case from the oven, allow to cool a little, then spread with the filling. Return the tart to the oven and bake for another 20–25 minutes, until the filling is set and the pastry crisp and golden. Leave to cool.

6 Finish with a layer of icing made by mixing the sifted confectioner's sugar with the brandy and enough water to achieve the consistency of heavy cream. Spread the icing over the tart with a palate knife dipped in hot water. Let it set for an hour or so and then decorate with walnut halves.

# croustade de pommes

## DOUBLE-CRUSTED APPLE TART

A specialty of south-western France, you'll find this tart on sale in the markets of the Périgord in the winter months, alongside the foie-gras goose. Crisp buttery layers of flaky pastry are used to enclose sliced apples soaked in Armagnac. The making of the pastry is a skill passed from mother to daughter: fine sheets of dough are stretched out on the fists rather than rolled. A technique of Arab origin employed in the making of both filo and the strudel doughs. The method requires that the layers be separated from one another by a brushing of butter. Here, the technique is somewhere in between that used for a flaky pastry and a filo—an egg-dough (much like pasta) is spread with softened butter. You may, if you prefer, replace the pastry dough with sheets of bought filo—six layers of crust each will be sufficient for both top and bottom.

Serves 6

**2½lb yellow-fleshed apples
(Reinettes or Golden Delicious)
about 4 tablespoons Armagnac or brandy**

PASTRY
**3 cups all-purpose flour
½ teaspoon salt
2 eggs, lightly forked together
scant 2¼ sticks butter, softened
2 tablespoons goose fat or pure pork lard, melted
⅔ cup sugar
egg yolk and milk to glaze**

1 Peel, core, and slice the apples. Sprinkle with the Armagnac—
enough to perfume the apples rather than drown them—and
leave for 1–2 hours to absorb the liquor.

2 Meanwhile, make the pastry. You will need about ⅔ cup water.
Sift the flour and salt into a bowl. Make a well in the middle
and crack in the eggs. Pull the flour into the eggs with your
hands, working gradually from the edges, adding water as you
go, until you have a soft, smooth dough, exactly as if you were
making home-made pasta. Form the dough into a ball, cover with
plastic wrap and set it aside to rest for 30 minutes—long enough to
soften the gluten in the flour and make the dough more elastic.

3 Beat the butter until creamy and reserve. Roll or pat out the
dough to a thickness of ¼in. Spread with the softened butter,

leaving a rim of a finger's width around the edge. Fold the dough over itself in three—take one edge and fold a third of the dough over the middle, then take the opposite edge and fold the remaining third over the top.

4 Roll the dough out again—you will need to flour it well. Leave it to rest again for 10 minutes. Repeat the operation— folding and rolling—three times. Finally, cut the dough into 2 pieces and roll each out as thin as possible—paper-thin shows real skill. Leave to dry for 1 hour.

5 Preheat the oven to 350°F. Brush both sheets of pastry with melted goose fat or lard. Reserve one sheet and use the other to line a 10in tart pan. Trim off the excess and cut it into 3–4 sheets, then place these gently on top of the lining pastry to form layers.

6 Spread the apple slices in the tart, dusting with sugar as you go. Dampen the edges of the pie, and top with rest of the pastry, laid on in layers as before. Trim and neaten the edges, and glaze the top with a little egg yolk and milk, forked together to blend. Cut a little hole in the top for the steam to escape.

7 Bake the tart for 30–40 minutes, until the pastry is crisp and browned. As soon as the pie comes out of the oven, sprinkle it with a little sugar and extra Armagnac shaken from your fingers.

**NOTE** ~ For an open (single crust) tarte aux pommes, line a tart pan with sweet pastry, arrange sufficient apple slices to cover the base, laying them in concentric circles. Fork ⅔ cup light cream with 2 egg yolks and sweeten with a little sugar. Trickle this between the slices and bake as above.

In France's cities and major towns, the pâtisserie, provides the urban housewife with the sugary treats which are served on special occasions—by no means every day. Domestic cooks rarely bake, preferring to leave the sophisticated tarts, cakes, and pastries of the French tradition to the experts. Her country cousin, however, expects to order her tarts and cakes in advance from the baker who, in the villages and small towns of rural France, doubles as the pastry-chef. His bakings reflect the seasons.

Winter tarts in my local market town in the Languedoc were filled with a compote of prunes, or topped with a thick layer of sliced apples perfumed with cinnamon, or crammed with a syrupy tangle of nuts and raisins—deliciously crisp and caramelized in the heat of the wood-fired oven.

Whatever his choice, the scent which curled down the street would be sure to attract a queue of eager customers —if you hadn't ordered in advance, you took your chance. Everyone knew what to expect. The arrival of the first strawberries in the market told you there would be strawberry tarts in the baker. When the first white peaches appeared on the stalls, peach tarts—ivory slivers slashed with scarlet laid in concentric circles on a bed of creamy custard— would be sure to appear in the baker's window. At the end of summer there would be little individual tartlets, a mouthful apiece, filled with the dark-skinned hedgerow fruits of autumn—cassis (blackcurrant), mure (blackberry), prune (sauvage), sloes. Finally, as autumn drew down, there would be lemon tarts to be warmed through in the oven as a triumphant conclusion to Sunday's midday dinner.

# tarte au citron

## LEMON TART

These beautiful sharp-flavored lemon tarts were a winter specialty of my local pâtisserie when I lived in the Languedoc. Tuesday was market day and the scent of citrus oil and warm butter would mingle with that of the blossom on the lemon trees that provided shade for the stall holders.

∽

Serves 8

1½ cups all-purpose flour
1 teaspoon salt
½ cup superfine sugar
1 stick butter, well chilled
2 egg yolks

FILLING
1 stick sweet butter, melted
4 lemons
½ cup superfine sugar
5 eggs

1 You will need a 10in tart pan, preferably with a removable base. Sift the flour into a bowl with the salt and sugar. Make a well in the middle of the flour mixture and grate in the cold butter. Mix lightly with a knife.

2 Beat the egg yolks with 1 tablespoon water and work them into the flour mixture with the tips of your fingers. Gather the mixture into a ball of fairly soft dough. If you need a little more water to make a soft dough, sprinkle in the minimum. Knead lightly and gently for a short time—this is a very rich pastry and liable to oil. Wrap the dough in plastic wrap or cover with a clean cloth and leave in a cool place for 30 minutes.

3 Preheat the oven to 400°F. Flour a board and roll out the pastry dough into a circle to fit the tart pan. Lay the pastry in the pan, easing it into the corners. Line with foil, weight with a handful of dried beans and bake for 12–15 minutes to set the pastry. Remove from the oven and take out the foil and beans. Leave to cool a little.

4 Reduce the oven temperature to 350°F. For the filling, whisk the eggs and sugar together lightly. Grate the zest from 1 lemon and squeeze the juice from all 4 lemons. Fold the zest, juice, and butter into the eggs. Immediately pour the filling into the tart case and put it in the oven to bake for 25 minutes, until the pastry is crisp and the filling perfectly set.

# *tarte aux fraises*

## STRAWBERRY TART

There can be nothing more deliciously summery than ripe strawberries embedded in a creamy pillow of custard spread on a base of crisp, buttery pastry. It really is worth making your own shortcrust rather than using bought pastry. When making pastry, keep everything very cool—hands, utensils, ingredients—and if possible use a marble slab for rolling. The colder the ingredients, the lighter the pastry, so pop the butter in the freezer first if it's a hot day. Should the custard scramble—perish the thought—tip it straight in the blender with a tablespoon of cold milk and whiz until smooth. Alternative fillings are fresh raspberries, black currants, peach slices, apricot halves or pitted cherries—choose an appropriate jam for the finishing glaze. Always assemble fresh fruit tarts at the last minute to make sure the pastry remains crisp and the fruit plump and bright.

Serves 10–12

**1½lb strawberries**

RICH SHORTCRUST PASTRY
**1½ cups all-purpose flour**
**pinch of salt**
**1 stick butter, well chilled**
**1 tablespoon superfine sugar**

CRÈME PÂTISSIÈRE
**2½ cups full-cream milk**
**4 egg yolks**
**4 tablespoons superfine sugar**
**1 heaped tablespoon flour**
**½ stick butter**
**a dash of Cointreau or fruit brandy (optional)**

TO FINISH
**2–3 tablespoons sieved strawberry or raspberry conserve**

❧

1 Pick over the strawberries and set aside. Make the pastry: sift the flour into a cool bowl with the salt. Grate in the cold butter and toss lightly—or use a knife to cut the butter into the flour instead of grating it. Rub the butter in lightly with your fingertips until the mixture looks like fine bread crumbs. Mix in the sugar.

2 Working with the fingers of one hand only, add 2–3 tablespoons very cold water—just enough water to form a ball. The dough should be firm but not damp, so you may need more or less water —it depends on the weather and the water content of the butter.

3 Transfer the pastry to a lightly floured board or marble slab, pat it with a floured rolling pin to flatten, and roll out to fit a 10in tart pan with a removable base—fluted is prettiest. Using the rolling pin as a support, lift the pastry and lay it in the tart pan. Trim the excess, leaving a generous lip to allow for shrinkage. Lay the trimmings around the rim to make a thicker edge (dampen it first). If the tart case tears anywhere, patch it with a scrap of pastry, dampened with a finger. Prick the base with a fork, line with foil, and chill for 30 minutes.

4 Preheat the oven to 375°F. Sprinkle a few dried beans or rice on the foil in the tart (not too many—just enough to weight it down). Bake for 15 minutes, remove the foil and beans, and bake for another 10 minutes, until the pastry is crisp and golden.

5 Meanwhile make the crème pâtissière. Put the milk, egg yolks, superfine sugar, flour, and butter in a blender and process thoroughly—the butter will make the mixture a little lumpy, but no matter. Pour into a heavy-based pan and whisk over a gentle heat until thick—do not let the custard boil for more than 1–2 minutes, just enough to cook the flour.

6 Whisk in the Cointreau or fruit brandy, if using, and tip the custard into a cold bowl. Leave to cool—the butter will solidify and help to thicken the custard.

7 To assemble the tart, remove the edge of the pan, but leave the base in place and spread the custard in the cooled tart. Top with the scarlet fruit. Melt the jam or jelly with its own volume of water and use to glaze the fruit.

" *I strongly believe that culinary love
is not about having a French
Passport, but about what you feel.* "

**Albert Roux,** contemporary chef and restaurateur

# *tarte tatin*

## UPSIDE-DOWN APPLE TART

The demoiselles Tatin, two spinster ladies who kept the station hotel in Lamotte-Beuvron near Orleans at the end of the nineteenth century, achieved culinary immortality with the upside-down apple pie which bears their name. For the pastry, I've suggested a lightly sweetened shortcrust—*pâte brisée*—but feel free to substitute a buttery puff pastry, *pâte feuilletée* (see page 294). Tarte tatin is lovely with thick crème fraîche or a crème anglaise (see page 266).

Serves 6

2¼ cups all-purpose flour
1 tablespoon confectioner's sugar
1¼ sticks butter, softened
1 egg

### FILLING
2¼lb yellow-fleshed apples
(Reinettes or Golden Delicious)
1 stick sweet butter
4 tablespoons superfine sugar
1 teaspoon ground cinnamon

1 Make the pastry first. Sift the flour with the confectioner's sugar. Chop the butter, add to the flour, and rub it in lightly with fingertips until the mixture looks like fine bread crumbs.

2 Fork up the egg with a little water and a pinch of salt, and work the liquid into the flour and butter lightly until you have a ball of dough—you may need a little more water. Do not overwork the dough. Form it into a ball, cover with plastic wrap and set aside for 30 minutes—or longer—in a cool place.

3 Preheat the oven to 375°F. Peel, quarter, and slice the apples (not too finely). Spread 1 tablespoon of the butter over the base of a 10in square flameproof baking pan, and sprinkle with 2 tablespoons of the sugar. Caramelize this sugar and butter over a high heat—do not let it burn.

4 Layer the apple slices in the pan, sprinkling with cinnamon and the remaining sugar, and dotting with scraps of butter.

5 Roll out the pastry to cover the apples comfortably with a generous flap to spare all round. Lay the pastry over the apples and tuck the flap between the apples and the pan to give an edge when the tart is unmolded.

6 Bake for about 25 minutes, until the pastry is nicely crisped and golden. Wait for 5 minutes before you tip the tart out, bottom side up (inverting it with a platter) so that the pastry ends up underneath.

# madeleines

## LITTLE BUTTER CAKES

**M**adeleines are little shell-shaped cakes of the perfect
size to hold between finger and thumb. They are just
right for dipping in an infusion of lime-blossom or verveine
(verbena), or a chilled glass of mint or orange syrup diluted
with well-water—the essence, in other words, of a lazy
afternoon in the shade of the wisteria terrace in Proustian high
summer. For perfection, you need madeleine molds, a special
baking tray indented with shallow shell-shaped cups, though the
mixture can just as well be baked in any individual cake or tart
tins, though these should be shallow rather than deep.

Makes about 30

**butter for greasing the tins**
**1 stick sweet butter, softened**
**1 cup superfine sugar**
**1¾ cups all-purpose flour**
**1 teaspoon baking powder**
**6 eggs**
**1 tablespoon orange-blossom water or orange juice**

1   Preheat the oven to 400°F and butter madeleine tins or small shallow patty tins. Beat the butter with the sugar until light and white—use a wooden spoon, electric beater or food processor.

2   Sift the flour with the baking powder and set aside. Crack the eggs one by one into the butter and sugar mixture, beating thoroughly between each addition until well blended. As you add the last couple of eggs you may need to sprinkle in a spoonful of flour to keep the mixture from splitting.

3   Using a metal spoon, fold in the remaining flour and the orange-blossom water or orange juice. Drop teaspoons of the mixture into the buttered madeleine tins.

4   Transfer to the oven and bake for 8–10 minutes, until the cakes have filled the tins completely and are firm, well-risen and browned. Allow to cool a little, then transfer to a rack. Store in an airtight tin when perfectly cool.

# *babas au rhum*

## RUM BABAS

This decadent little dessert has been popular in the brasseries of Paris since the days when Toulouse-Lautrec kept company with the demoiselles of Montmartre. While the recipe—buttery little yeast-raised buns drenched in rum-flavored syrup—is of Polish origin, it speaks to the French soul of the days of Empire. Rum is produced in the French West Indies, the birthplace of Napolean's Empress Josephine.

∽

Makes 12 babas

2 tablespoons raisins
4 tablespoons rum
3 cups bread flour
½ teaspoon salt
1oz fresh yeast/½oz dried yeast/1 packet easy-blend yeast
⅔ cup milk, warmed
2 tablespoons sugar
½ stick sweet butter, melted, plus extra for greasing tins
2 eggs

TO FINISH
4 cups stock syrup (see page 260)
⅔ cup dark rum
crème fraîche

1 Put the raisins to soak and swell in the rum for an hour or so.

2 Sift the flour and salt into a warm bowl. If using fresh yeast, blend it to a liquid in half the warm milk, make a well in the flour, pour in the yeasted milk, sprinkle with a handful of the flour, then set aside for 15 minutes in a warm place for the yeast to begin to work. If using dried yeast, sprinkle it over half the milk and leave to dissolve for a few minutes, before stirring it and pouring with the flour as for fresh yeast. If using easy-bake yeast, mix it into the flour—no need for sponge-setting.

3 Add the sugar and the rest of the milk (or all the milk, if using easy-bake yeast). Work the wet ingredients into the dry to make a soft, smooth dough, leaving any unabsorbed flour loose. Work in the melted butter and the eggs, taking up the unabsorbed flour as you work: persist until all is absorbed, when the dough will be soft and sloppy. Work in the raisins and their soaking rum.

4 Brush 12 individual molds with melted butter. Divide the dough between the molds. Set to rise in a warm place for 1–2 hours, until the dough has risen to the top of the molds.

5 Preheat the oven to 400°F. Bake the babas for 15–20 minutes, until well-risen, brown, and firm to the finger. Transfer to a rack to cool completely.

6 Bring the sugar syrup to the boil in a large pan. Place the rack holding the babas over a plate to catch drippings of syrup. Drop the babas into the syrup a few at a time, then wait until no more bubbles rise before you remove them with a draining spoon. Transfer the babas back to the rack.

7 Allow to cool a little, then trickle with the rum. Spoon the drippings over the babas as they cool. Serve with dollops ofcrème fraîche.

**NOTES ~**
• If using easy blend dried yeast, mix it with the flour and use milk that is hand-hot rather than lukewarm, mixing in the whole quantity in one go. No need to set the sponge.
• For an instant version of the babas, use ready made brioches and add the raisins to the soaking syrup instead of baking them in the dough.

*It was in France that I first learned about food. And that even the selection of a perfect pear, a ripe piece of Brie, the freshest butter, the highest quality cream were as important as how the dish you were going to be served was actually cooked.*

**Robert Carrier,** contemporary chef and restaurateur

# reine de saba

## ALMOND AND CHOCOLATE CAKE

Light, buttery and moist, this dark crumbed cake—queen of Sheba—is flavored with rum imported from the sugar plantations of French West Indies. France's former colonies are actually overseas departments with the right to send representatives to parliament in Paris. It's good with vanilla ice cream and wild strawberries.

Serves 6–8

**butter and flour for greasing and dusting**
**7 squares dark bitter chocolate**
**1 tablespoon golden or dark rum, preferably St. James's**
**1¼ sticks butter**
**¾ cup superfine sugar**
**5 eggs, separated**
**1 cup ground almonds**

⟜⟳

1 Preheat the oven to 350°F. Butter a 7in square cake pan and dust with flour—if using a round pan, choose one of 8in diameter. The cake will be easier to remove if you line the base with non-stick baking parchment.

2 Melt the chocolate with the rum, butter, and sugar in a bowl set over a pan of simmering water. Remove from the heat and allow to cool a little.

3 Meanwhile, whisk the egg whites until they hold soft peaks. Beat the egg yolks into the still-runny chocolate. Mix in the ground almonds. Then fold in the whisked whites, adding only a little at first so that the mixture lightens and can accept the rest.

4 Spread the mixture in to the prepared pan. Bake for 40–50 minutes, until well risen and firm to the finger. Leave to cool before removing from the pan. If the cake cracks on top, that is part of its charm—fix it with a sprinkle of confectioner's sugar.

# langues de chat

## FINGER COOKIES

Literally, cats' tongues, these are crisp little cookies for eating with creamy desserts or ice creams, or just for dipping into a chilled glass of Sauternes or any of France's cellarful of delicious sweet wines. Good too, with one of the aperitifs French housewives keep on the shelf for special occasions: home-made vin d'orange, one of the herb-flavored vermouths—Noilly or Chambéry—or a drop of cassis diluted with champagne.

Makes about 24 cookies

**butter for greasing and flour for dusting**
**1 stick sweet butter, softened**
**⅔ cup superfine sugar**
**a knife tip of vanilla seeds or ¼ teaspoon real vanilla essence**
**2 eggs**
**1 cup all-purpose flour**

1 Preheat the oven to 450°F. Butter a couple of baking sheets and dust with a little flour. Beat the softened butter with the sugar until light and white, adding the vanilla—use a wooden spoon or a food processor.

2 Beat in the eggs, one at a time. Fold in the flour with a metal spoon, turning the mixture over to blend the ingredients. Spoon the mixture into a piping bag fitted with a plain round nozzle and pipe fingers of mixture about 2in long, leaving plenty of room between each to allow for spreading.

3 Bake for 5–6 minutes, until the edges have browned and the middles are firm and golden. Remove and transfer carefully to a baking rack to crisp and cool. Store in an airtight container when cold.

# the french storecupboard

## EVERYDAY CHARCUTERIE

You'll find plenty of regional variety in the charcuterie, the cured-pork shop which provides the French cook with the basic hors d'œuvres as well as other little delicacies which need minimum culinary attention. No meal however modest or grand—from presidential banquet to school dinner—can be considered complete without its little appetizer, its palate-awakener—a sliver of saucisson, a scrap of jambon cru.

*Jambon cru (de Bayonne or de campagne):* country ham— salt-cured air-dried ham eaten raw, a light smoking makes it different from Italy's prosciutto and Spain's serrano. Usually served with a little pat of sweet butter.

*Saucisson sec:* the French version of Italian salami: salt-cured air-dried all-meat sausage designed to be sliced and eaten raw. Individual appearance and flavor depends on the shape and size of the intestine into which the meat is stuffed, the proportion of fat to meat and the spices and herbs used to season the mix.

*Cervelas:* a short, thick frankfurter-like boiling sausage which can also be grilled—good wrapped in a galette bretonne (see page 284), a pancake made with buckwheat flour.

*Saucisse de Toulouse:* an all-meat pork sausage for frying or grilling. Uncured as well as cured French sausages never contain rusk and are usually spiced rather than flavored with herbs.

*Boudin noir:* blood-sausage or black pudding, precooked and finished by grilling or frying; delicious fried in butter with apples.

*Boudin blanc:* white pudding, a delicate poaching-sausage (though it can also be grilled) made with white meat—pork or chicken—pounded smooth with pork-fat, eggs, and cream but no blood. Exquisite with pommes de terre mousselines (see page 94)—fluffy mashed potato.

## STORECUPBOARD FISH

*Anchois en conserve:* In Provence, anchovies, cheap and plentiful in Mediterranean waters, are eaten fresh as well as preserved in salt, the form in which, along with garlic and olive oil, they define the cooking of Provence. While canned is the form in which they are most widely recognized—filleted, de-salted and preserved under oil—in Provence they are sold direct from the barrel, when they will need de-salting and de-whiskering—to prepare, brush off the salt-grains and soak in a little milk, then remove the hairy little bones by running your thumb down the spine. To prepare as an anchoïade—dipping sauce for raw vegetables—crush 3–4 anchovy fillets and a sliver or two of garlic into $^{2}/_{3}$ cup warm olive oil. When added to a fish soup or sauce, they melt into the background, subtly heightening the flavor. Quality counts. When serving them as an hors d'œuvre, leave them in the tin with the top rolled down and the label proudly displayed so that all may admire your choice.

*Morue:* salt-cod, bacalhau, was for many centuries the fast-day food of Roman Catholic inhabitants of the shores of the Mediterranean – a curious situation since the fish itself is only found in the Atlantic. The trade was particularly valuable during the Middle Ages, a time when more than half the year was fasting—meatless days included Wednesdays as well as Fridays, the Eves of all saints days and the forty days preceeding Christmas as well as the Lenten fast. In response to what was intended as deprivation, the resourceful cooks of France, unwilling to eat something which didn't taste good, invented dishes so delicious they are eaten to this day. In French markets around Christmas time, when salt-cod is the traditional dish of the fasting supper which preceeds the feast itself, you can buy your morue ready-soaked.

To prepare salt-cod from scratch, choose a piece of middle-cut, pale but not too white (a sign of artificial bleaching), with no trace of pink. Soak it in several changes of water for 36–48 hours until it rehydrates and softens. Cover with fresh water and cook in gently simmering water—do not allow it to boil—for 15–20 minutes, until tender. It can now be prepared as if it were fresh fish: in Provence they like it sauced with tomato, olives, onion, and olive oil. In the Rouergue, where nut oils replace the olive oil of the south, they like it beaten into mashed potatoes with walnut oil.

## OILS AND COOKING FATS

It is possible to divide the cooking of France into three broad bands according to the inhabitant's preference for cooking with olive oil, goose fat or butter. The inhabitants of the southern regions—Provence and the eastern Languedoc where olive trees thrive—cook with olive oil. For la France Profonde—the central heartland from the Pyranees through the Massif Centrale—the natural choice is goose fat. For the northerners—the inhabitants of Normandy, Brittany, the territories bordering Germany and Belgium, as well as the rich farmlands of the valley of the Loire —the choice is butter. In those areas—particularly Berry— where olive trees cannot thrive and the taste for butter or goose fat is not strongly developed, nut oils, particularly walnut, replace the olive oil. Although no longer so sharply defined, the distinctions apply to this day.

## HERBS IN COMMON USE

Tarragon, the quintessentially French herb, is irreplaceable in butter, cream, and wine sauces and has a particular affinity with white meats—chicken and veal, the specialities of the rich farmlands. Rosemary, thyme, savory, and several other localized members of thyme family are the flavoring herbs of Provence; these, when grown in harsh conditions on Mediterranean hillsides, lose none of their pungency or even their weight when dried, the form in which they are most fragrant (do not bother with the soft-leafed stuff sold 'fresh' in cellophane packets). Along with marjoram and bay, they have an affinity with pork, beef, and game. The Provençale herb jar includes orange zest— finely pared and dehydrated to intensify the flavor—for adding to slow-cooked stews. Central France likes the milder mixes of mustard including those of Dijon and Bordeaux, while northern France has a taste for chives.

In addition to herbs, French storecupboards are usually stocked with a jar or two of dried fungi, a seasonal treat in a form available throughout the year. Only a handful of the wild-gathered fungi which are eaten fresh are suitable for dehydration: of the autumn mushrooms, chanterelles, and cèpes are suitable; the best, however, is the morel, a spring mushroom which, though excellent fresh, is even better when dried. As for the truffle family, the black or Périgord truffle (also found in considerable quantity in Upper Provence) is sold "en conserve", tinned or jarred, but it's not a patch on the real thing. And don't bother with the truffle oil, either—something unrecognizable happens to the flavor, even if it's not a chemical copy. If you have reason to wish to preserve a truffle, buy your own, mash it up with butter and pop it in the freezer.

# useful conversion charts

Use this basic guide for converting measurements from metric and imperial to cup measures. Volumes are standard. Weight can vary according to the density of the ingredients, so the basic ingredients should be used as a rough guide.

| USING CUP AND SPOON MEASURES | |
| --- | --- |
| All cup and spoon measures should be level (unless otherwise stated). | |
| ¼ teaspoon | 1.25ml |
| ½ teaspoon | 2.5ml |
| 1 teaspoon | 5ml |
| 1 tablespoon | 15ml |

| LIQUID MEASURES | | |
| --- | --- | --- |
| Cup | Metric | Imperial |
| ¼ cup | 60ml | 2fl oz |
| 1 cup | 250ml | 8fl oz |
| 1¼ cups | 300ml | ½ pint |
| 1½ cups | 350ml | 12fl oz |
| 1¾ cups | 400ml | 14fl oz |
| 2 cups | 475ml | 16fl oz |
| 2½ cups | 600ml | 1 pint |
| 3 cups | 750ml | 1¼ pints |
| 4 cups | 1 litre | 1¾ pints |

| WEIGHTS | | | |
| --- | --- | --- | --- |
| Imperial | Metric | Imperial | Metric |
| ¼lb | 100g | 1lb 2oz | 500g |
| 6oz | 175g | 1¼lb | 575g |
| ½lb | 225g | 1½lb | 675g |
| 12oz | 350g | 1¾lb | 800g |
| 1lb | 450g | 2¼lb | 1kg |

## OVEN TEMPERATURES

| °F | °C | Gas |
|---|---|---|
| 225 | 110 | ¼ |
| 250 | 120 | ½ |
| 275 | 140 | 1 |
| 300 | 150 | 2 |
| 325 | 160 | 3 |
| 350 | 180 | 4 |
| 375 | 190 | 5 |
| 400 | 200 | 6 |
| 425 | 220 | 7 |
| 450 | 230 | 8 |
| 475 | 250 | 9 |

## BASIC INGREDIENTS
### Cup and Weight Equivalents

| | |
|---|---|
| Bread crumbs, dry | 1 cup = 2½oz / 65g |
| Bread crumbs, fresh | 1 cup = 2oz / 50g |
| Butter | 1 cup = 8oz / 225g<br>2 tablespoons = 2oz / 50g |
| Cheese, grated Cheddar | 1 cup = 4oz / 100g |
| Confectioner's sugar | 1 cup = 4oz / 100g |
| Cornstarch | 1 cup = 8oz / 225g |
| Couscous | 1 cup = 6oz / 175g |
| Cream cheese, ricotta | 1 cup = 8oz / 225g |
| Flour | 1 cup = 4oz / 100g |
| Honey | 1 cup = 8oz / 225g |
| Parmesan cheese, grated | 1 cup = 3oz / 75g |
| Peas, frozen | 1 cup = 4oz / 100g |
| Rice, long grain types | 1 cup = 7oz / 200g |
| Sugar, granulated<br>or superfine | 1 cup (generous) = 8oz / 225g<br>1 cup (scant) = 7oz / 200g |

# INDEX

Entries in *italics* refer to
recipe names

Hailed by food critics internationally, Elisabeth has won a
series of awards for her unique, intelligent, and engaging
writing. She has published more than a dozen books including
MQP's *Sacred Food*—for which she was awarded the coveted
Gourmand World Cook Book Award in 2001—and two
successful novels and two autobiographies-with-recipes. In
2001 she received the Glenfiddich Magazine Writer of the
Year award for her work in *Waitrose Food Illustrated*.
Elisabeth currently lives on a hill farm in Wales.